To Bill,
　　　from Renée & Douglas,
　　　　　　Xmas 1947.

EDWARD ELGAR
MEMORIES OF A VARIATION

EDWARD AND ALICE ELGAR

At Garmisch, Bavarian Highlands. About 1894

EDWARD ELGAR

MEMORIES OF A VARIATION

Mrs. Richard Powell

SECOND EDITION

GEOFFREY CUMBERLEGE
OXFORD UNIVERSITY PRESS
London   New York   Toronto
1947

109614

OXFORD UNIVERSITY PRESS
AMEN HOUSE, E.C. 4
London Edinburgh Glasgow New York
Toronto Melbourne Cape Town Bombay
Calcutta Madras
GEOFFREY CUMBERLEGE
PUBLISHER TO THE UNIVERSITY

First Edition 1937
Second Edition 1947

PRINTED IN GREAT BRITAIN
1646.5582

To the Memory
of
A. J. J.

FOREWORD
TO THE SECOND EDITION

MOST of the new matter in this revised and enlarged edition was written in 1936–7, but was deleted for various personal reasons. For the same reasons many descriptions were modified, but are now given as originally written.

The chapter on the VARIATIONS is entirely new, and is illustrated with photographs of the thirteen friends to whom the work is dedicated, and a recently found portrait of the composer.

There is also a short chapter on the ENIGMA.

My thanks are due to the following for permission to quote from books and letters and to publish photographs: Sir Ivor Atkins, Mrs. Edith K. Baker, Father Vincent Baker, Sir Granville Bantock, The Rt. Hon. Earl Beauchamp, Mrs. Elgar-Blake, Mr. Eric Blom, Miss R. C. Burley, Miss Lilian Griffith, Dr. Percy Hull, Messrs. John Lane—The Bodley Head, Ltd., Messrs. Macmillan & Co., Mr. W. McNaught (Messrs. Novello & Co., Ltd.), Mr. Alexander Brent Smith, and Mrs. Arthur Trew. Also to Mr. Harold Connold, Photographer, of East Grinstead, for his interest and skilled work in reconditioning old photographs.

D. M. P.

September 1946

FOREWORD

IN writing a book such as this, which depends upon diaries, letters, and memories, one finds that it falls naturally into chronological sequence.

The principal difficulty has been to avoid turning it into something uncomfortably like an autobiography. To make the bits and scraps of which it is composed to some extent continuous, and to explain things in general, it has been necessary for me to appear more than I should wish.

My thanks are due to Mrs. Elgar-Blake and to Mrs. Hunter, as well as to the executors of the late Sir Edward Elgar, for permission to reprint letters to me from Sir Edward Elgar and Mr. A. J. Jaeger respectively; to Messrs. Reginald Haines, Histed, and Window and Groves for permission to use portraits by them; and to Miss May Grafton for permission to reproduce the photograph of Sir Edward taken in the study at Plâs Gwyn.

D. M. P.

April 1937

PREFACE

Woodend, Broadheath
near Worcester
Dec. 5th, 1936

MY DEAR DORA

You have given me the very pleasant task of bestowing my blessing on your reminiscences of what were, in spite of the difficulties and worries attendant on the life of a genius and the making of a career, such happy days. And I do it most willingly because I am grateful to you for this faithful and vivid picture of my parents. There is no such record except in the memories of those who were associated with them. You have also shown so beautifully the wonderful unselfishness and devotion of my Mother and the inspiration and help of 'Nimrod'.

I have been reduced to a condition of helplessness over the scenes you describe, of which I recall so many. Those who know anything of our home life will live them again with mingled tears and laughter—to those who do not it will come perhaps as a revelation that the home life of a genius could be so happy and spontaneous, and contain none of the freakish elements which for some unexplained reason are inevitably associated with it.

Yours affectionately

CARICE ELGAR-BLAKE

CONTENTS

FOREWORD TO SECOND EDITION   vii

FOREWORD   viii

PREFACE   ix

1895   1

FORLI   6

CRAEG LEA   14

PLÂS GWYN   63

'THE O.M.'   98

'MY FRIENDS PICTURED WITHIN'   100

THE ENIGMA   119

CONCLUSION   122

SEPTEMBER 1946   127

APPENDIX   129

INDEX   131

LIST OF ILLUSTRATIONS

EDWARD AND ALICE ELGAR, *photographed at Garmisch, in the Bavarian Highlands, about 1894* Frontispiece

LETTER FROM ELGAR *dated 12 March 1898* facing p. 4

SEAL 7

EDWARD ELGAR AND A. J. JAEGER *at Hasfield Court, Gloucester, September 1901* 37

LETTER FROM ELGAR, *as 'NANTY EWART', in the Spring of 1901* 38

LETTER FROM ELGAR *dated 10 October 1901* 39

LETTER FROM ELGAR *dated 15 October 1902* 50

SIR EDWARD ELGAR, *1904, from a photograph by Window and Groves* 62

PLÂS GWYN, *from a photograph by the author* 64

SIR EDWARD ELGAR, *1909, from a photograph taken at Plâs Gwyn by Miss May Grafton* 84

At the York Festival, 1910 90

SIR EDWARD ELGAR, O.M., *1911, from a portrait by Histed* 98

THE XIV VARIATIONS:—

    I. C. A. E., *from a photograph by Mr. Reginald Haines* 101

    II. H. D. S-P. *and* XII. B. G. N. 103

    III. R. B. T. *and* IV. W. M. B. 104

    V. R. P. A. *and* VI. Ysobel 106

    VII. Troyte *and* VIII. W. N. 108

    IX. Nimrod *and* X. Dorabella 111

    XI. G. R. S. (*in group*) 113

    XIII. (***) Romanza 114

    XIV. E. D. U., *from a photograph taken at Malvern by Miss Florence Burley* 116

LETTER FROM ELGAR *dated 17 December 1913.* 124

I FIRST met Edward Elgar on 6 December 1895. He and Mrs. Elgar came to Wolverhampton at the invitation of my stepmother. They came to luncheon, spent the afternoon, and had tea. My father had been made Rector of Wolverhampton in the spring of that year and in the following August he married Miss Mary Frances Baker, of Hasfield, near Gloucester. With Miss Baker came a very substantial addition in the furniture line to our large Rectory, and the connexion with her brought us a host of most delightful new friends.

Caroline Alice Roberts, daughter of General Sir Henry Gee Roberts, K.C.B., was one of a group of girl friends who studied geology with the Rev. William Samuel Symonds, Rector of Pendock, Worcestershire. They used to go fossil-hunting on the banks of the Severn, and my stepmother tells of the delightful times they had and what an interesting and dear friend Mr. Symonds was to all of them. They called him 'the Professor'. Later on Alice Roberts, who lived with her mother at Redmarley, took accompaniment lessons from a Mr. Elgar who was teacher of the violin at Worcester High School when Miss Ottley was headmistress.

'Dear Alice!' my stepmother said, 'How hard she worked at it. She nearly wore her fingers to the bone practising and I couldn't think what for. She would never have made a fine player.'

After the death of Lady Roberts, Alice went abroad for a time and then settled down at a little house in Malvern Link called Ripple Lodge. There she went on with her accompaniment lessons, and before long the mystery was solved—she and Mr. Elgar became engaged to be married. They came over to see Miss Baker at Hasfield and he was terribly shy and quiet! They were married in 1889 and went to live in London, in Marloes Road. Miss Baker stayed with them there. Later that year they had a house lent to them in College Road, Upper

Norwood, and in the following spring they moved on to a house in Avonmore Road. During this time Mr. Elgar took full advantage of the Opera Season at Covent Garden and was often seen 'up among the gods', especially on a Wagner night. Two years after the birth of their daughter, Carice (now Mrs. Elgar-Blake), they stayed with Miss Baker at Hasfield. It was summer time and very hot. He used to bring in hedgehogs from the woods and feed them in the house. He sat in the strawberry bed and wished that some one would bring him champagne in a bedroom jug. As he was deep in ideas for *The Black Knight* this is not surprising.[1]

In 1892 Miss Baker took them to Bayreuth. They heard *Parsifal, Tannhäuser, Die Meistersinger*; and *Parsifal* for a second time the night before they left. He was wild with enthusiasm and delight. From Bayreuth they went to Heidelberg and then on into the Bavarian Highlands.

I once got him on to the subject of that Bayreuth Festival—years later, sitting on a bank looking at the Severn.

She did give us a splendid time—I called her 'the Mascotte'—did you know that? I made her stamp and post the manuscript of *The Black Knight* when it went off to Novello's. We posted it at Heidelberg. I said she would bring me luck and so she did.

I seem to have digressed somewhat, but picture us now, my stepmother and me, tramming up to the station at Wolverhampton to meet them, on Friday 6 December 1895. The train came in and, of course, not having seen one another for an age, the two friends fell upon each other and Mr. Elgar was left for me to look after. I quickly found out that music was the last thing he wanted to talk about. I think we talked about football. He wanted to know if I ever saw the Wolverhampton Wanderers play, and when he heard that our house was a stone's throw from their ground he was quite excited.

'Can't we go and see a match to-day?'

---

[1] E. E. always spoke of the theme at Scene 4, Letter G, as the 'Perrier Jouet' theme.

'There isn't one, I'm afraid; it's a Friday.'

'I shall come again on a Saturday. Will you take me to a match?'

He came into the drawing-room before luncheon: 'Hullo, there's the black piano! Let's see how its inside has stood the move.'

Although I had not left school very long I had heard a number of good pianists, but I had never heard anything quite like this. He didn't play like a pianist, he almost seemed to play like a whole orchestra. It sounded full without being loud and he contrived to make you hear other instruments joining in. It fascinated me then and always. But how difficult it was to turn over for him! When it came to playing from his own manuscripts you often saw nothing but a few pencilled notes and a mark or two, when he was playing something tremendous—full orchestra and chorus perhaps.

'Well, why don't you turn over?'

In time I think I became rather clever at it, and loved nothing better. When I came to know them very well it was the usual thing, almost directly after I arrived, for me to slide into a seat by the piano ready to turn over with just the greeting, 'There you are. That's all right.'

But to return.

After luncheon that first day we all went to the drawing-room for coffee and he took hold of a high-backed wooden chair to bring it forward—and its back came off.

'Here's another old friend and its back still comes off. Why don't you mend it?'

I said it was a job which got put off to another day.

'Well, this is the day. Got any tools?'

So, after coffee, bearing with us the chair, we departed to my sitting-room and started on it.

'Now clearly understand,' he said, 'if this is a success *I* mended it; if it's a failure *you* did it.'

That, I think, sealed our friendship.

But it was not until October in the following year, when

3

they were with us for a long week-end, that we were able to go to a football match. It all delighted him. The dense crowd flowing down the road like a river; the roar of welcome as the rival teams came on to the ground; the shouts of men calling to their player-friends by their Christian names—usually considerably shortened; the staccato 'Aw!' at a mishap (a most remarkable sound from a crowd of sixty thousand); and the deafening roar that greeted a goal. He was much taken with the names of some of the players—particularly Malpas, a famous member of the 'Wolves' at that time. I have known him say when we met:

'There you are. How's Malpas?'—a question I was not always able to answer.

After a match in February 1898 he was most keen that I should send him a local paper with an account of it, which I subsequently did. The reporter used a characteristic expression in describing the culmination of a fine piece of tactical work: 'he banged the leather for goal.'

This brought a letter from E. E.[1] by return of post in which he had set the words to music, so greatly did they take his fancy. This letter goes on:

I have a mug—not the one with the moustache, which you have seen (and heard)—but a brand new one, to drink out of, made at Hanley & presented to me with my name on & an extract from K. Olaf. Yours ever   ED. ELGAR.

Late in the afternoon of 17 October 1896, after a football match, E. E. went up to Stoke to take a final chorus rehearsal of *King Olaf*, which was to be produced at the Hanley Festival a fortnight later. He came back late that night very full of it all; the rehearsal had evidently gone well. He played *Olaf* and other things nearly all Sunday. It was lovely, and I felt a sort of new world opening out before me of which I had never dreamed.

Quite a large party of us—relations and friends—went up

[1] Most of his friends appear to have alluded to Edward Elgar as 'E. E.'

4

M'c'n

Mar 12

(1898)

Dear Miss!

Many thanks for the

letter etc. I need

still joy

for that Hanley Festival and heard *King Olaf,* and I think it was a really fine performance. In the vocal score which I took with me that day, signed by the composer, I put many of the press notices which followed. Some of them are interesting to read now:

To sum up a necessarily hurried judgement, 'King Olaf' is a work of high importance, one which should turn expectant eyes upon its composer as a musician within whose reach, apparently, lies no common distinction. (*The Times,* 30 October 1896.)

Generally speaking the cantata surpassed all expectations. It reached a very high level indeed, . . . one of the numerous critics even going so far as to assert that while we have now in this country plenty of composers of great merit, Mr. Elgar is the first among them who has shown distinct genius. (*Staffordshire Sentinel,* 31 October 1896.)

Fortunately I kept a diary in those days and, still more fortunately, the diaries have been kept. Part of the entry for Friday, 30 October 1896, reads:

'Mr. Elgar came and saw us in the interval. Went to Choral Symphony in the evening. Mr. E. sat with me most of the time.'

Any one who has sat next E. E. during a performance which he was enjoying knows what it is to be thrilled, and also knows what it is to have an arm black and blue with bruises next day. I have done it many times. With practice one learnt to shift imperceptibly now and then so that the position of the grip varied.

FORLI

THE Elgars were living at Forli, North Malvern, when I first knew them. I think they had gone there late in 1891. On 17 August 1896 my stepmother and I went down to Malvern for the day with the Choirmen's outing from St. Peter's, Wolverhampton. We left that party to the care of others and betook ourselves to the Elgars for luncheon.

Forli was a semi-detached house in Alexandra Road and it only took us a few minutes to walk there from Malvern Link station. There was a lawn in front of the two houses divided into two parts—one had a lawn-tennis court, and there was a small tree which gave a modicum of shade on the other. The whole area was supposed to be shared by the occupants of the two houses. There was a fine view of the hills from the front of the house, and the North Hill stood up like a huge hump and seemed a good deal closer than it really was. They had called the house Forli after the Italian painter, Melozzo da Forli, who painted angels playing instruments.

It was a hot day and on the lawn in front of the house was a small bell-tent. E. E., in his shirt-sleeves, was writing at a little table.

'You can't come in here—it's private.'

Hot and stuffy too, I thought, but he seemed to like it. After luncheon he suggested a walk and we spent the afternoon on the North Hill. How lovely it was up there! The wonderful air and the view—I had never been to Malvern before. He pointed out various places and landmarks and I said admiringly:

'You're as good as a map!'

'Better,' he said. 'We'll do the Worcestershire Beacon next time you come, only you must stay, not flit like this.'

He was as good as his word and on another occasion we had another lovely afternoon on the top of the world, 'far away from smoky towns', as he remarked. He soon found that I was as keen on maps and map-reading as he was. Also he added

6

'MY PARCEL-POST SEAL'

to the interest of these expeditions by bringing in all sorts of stories about the various places that could be seen, and many historical details too. I found him a veritable mine of information. Sometimes he used to tease me by inventing historical 'facts':

'Oh, but surely——' I once began cautiously—

'I wondered when you'd stop me; I thought perhaps you hadn't done any history at your school!'

On 5 March 1897 I had a letter from E. E. and at the back of the envelope was a red seal about the size of a half-crown.

Forli Malvern March 4

Dear Miss Penny

Here is some locomotive learning; so much nicer than mouldy music.

Alice tells me you are warbling wigorously in Worcester wunce a week (alliteration archaically Norse).

I am very glad, but on second thoughts, as I have never heard you sing I am not sure: but perhaps some day if you are not rushing away I might arrange to show you over the Cathedral organ, K. John's tomb and the Dane's skin: (the Dane is dead).

By the way I have taken to 'die-sinking' as a recreation: here on the back of this is my parcel-post seal: I have to register all my MSS & they will not give a receipt unless they are sealed: so I put this on that my works may be Esily distinguished.

Kindest regards to everybody

Believe me Sincerely yours

EDWARD ELGAR

E. E. began to be keen on kite-flying about that time and when they both came to Wolverhampton in the following July we drove over to Boscobel and flew kites in the field near King Charles's Oak. That was a very jolly day. They both enjoyed seeing Boscobel and went all over the old house.

Thinking how I could amuse our guest I asked him, when they arrived the previous day, if he would care to go down to a friend's house close to the Dunstall Park Race-course and see a bit of the Meeting that was taking place next day. I thought we could manage to fit it in before the proposed Boscobel excursion. We had a standing invitation to take visitors to see the racing; the white railings of the course were what my father called a 'biscuit-toss' from the garden fence. Leaving the rest of the party to finish luncheon in a more leisurely fashion E. E. and I departed post-haste down to Dunstall Hall by tram, and we were able to see three races before we had to come away again to join our party at the drive gates, on the way to Boscobel.

'This is what I call eating one's cake and having it,' remarked E. E. as we got into the carriage.

(It is curious to look back at that incident. It was not until over twenty years later that I read, in various books and papers, that E. E. was greatly interested in horses and horse-racing! Apart from the incident just described, neither horses nor racing were ever mentioned, so far as I know, in the Elgar household during the fifteen years of my close acquaintance with them. I think, really, that it was only after the death of Lady Elgar that racing was one of the interests that he took up by way of relaxation or, as we should say to-day, escapism.

It was much the same with dogs. I never found out that E. E. was particularly fond of dogs, and they had no dog in the house during Lady Elgar's lifetime. She was not a 'doggy' person; her love was for birds, but it was not till they went to Hereford in 1904 that I found *that* out. The veranda round two sides of the house at Plâs Gwyn became a sort of birds' hotel and restaurant! They fed, drank, and bathed in the veranda and roosted in the overhanging honeysuckle and jasmine. They became wonderfully tame and the Lady loved them all.)

They stayed with us for five days on that occasion and we had music at all hours: *Lux Christi, Scenes from the Bavarian Highlands,* and lots of sketches for *Caractacus.* I remember how much I liked the 'Bavarians' and, after he had played the Lullaby (*In Hammersbach*), I could not help interrupting, 'That's lovely—I should like to dance to that.'

'I wish you would: I'll play it again.'

An interruption fortunately gave me time to escape and slip into another frock and also to think out something. (I used to amuse myself by inventing dances rather in the Maud Allan style of later years.) When I got back into the drawing-room peace once more reigned and we tried it out. He seemed much pleased and we did it again, trying bits where steps had not quite fitted in and so on. So much did he like it that I was called upon to 'come and dance Hammersbach' on several occasions at Malvern.

E. E. demanded to be taken over a Rope Walk one day and, when we returned home, played the most comic twisty music till I had to beg him to stop; it made me feel quite giddy.

In February 1898 the Elgars came to Wolverhampton for nearly a week, during which *King Olaf* was splendidly done at Birmingham, and not so splendidly done, alas, by the Wolverhampton Choral Society. I don't know how it was, except that after a brilliant final rehearsal in the presence of E. E. the previous evening all had gone so swimmingly and he had been so complimentary and we were all so cock-a-hoop, that a downfall was about due. These things happen sometimes. The same Society (before my time) had very successfully performed *The Black Knight* in 1895, and in years to come distinguished itself in the later, greater compositions.

That April I stayed at Forli for nearly a week and had the most hilarious time. There was a Worcester Philharmonic Concert, the first of many to which I went, followed by tea at the hospitable Mrs. Hyde's, in Foregate Street, where I made the acquaintance of many friends, several of whom were to be 'co-variants' (as E. E. called us) of mine: Miss Fitton, Miss Norbury, Mr. Arnold, and Mr. Troyte Griffith. Mr. Griffith came back to Forli with us to dinner that night, but I have in my diary 'Ninepin to dinner' (what impertinence!). It was a most uproarious evening.

When ten o'clock came Mrs. Elgar (as she was then) and I went off to bed, and left the two men in the study. It was so tantalizing to hear roars of laughter coming from next door. I used to lie awake and listen and wonder what it was all about. At last the study door opened and I heard them go downstairs and the front door was shut and bolted. Then E. E. went back into the study and began to play, and of course one could not possibly go to sleep then! How I longed to get up and tip-toe to the study door and listen! As it was not possible to hear the quiet parts distinctly it was all the more annoying, and also rather tiring, but I listened intently till it was over. This happened on more than one occasion.

I saw, for the first time, the poker-work design over the study fire-place, of which I had heard. I thought it was beautifully done and E. E. was very proud of his handiwork. It was a phrase from the *Walküre* 'fire music'. When they moved to Malvern Wells they took it with them and placed it over the study fire-place at Craeg Lea. It was not taken to Hereford.

Next day we went up to Birchwood, the cottage in the woods, north of the town, that the Elgars had recently taken. It was a lovely spot, though as I saw it for the first time in very early spring its full beauties were not to show themselves to me till later. We unpacked furniture that day and sorted things out.

There were only two sitting-rooms at Birchwood and the study was a tiny place. When a piano, a table, and two chairs were in it there was not more than room to turn round. When they first went up there they had a most comic little old piano. I played a few notes on it and it made a tinny little noise rather like a spinet.

'Surely he's not going to use this?'

'It does sound rather funny, dear Dora, but I assure you dear Edward makes it sound beautiful!'

'That's uncommonly clever of him!'

The next time I went there, however, I noticed that they had changed it for a more modern one—and there was even less room in the study.

In August that year I went to Birchwood for the day with a

cousin. She and I lunched with the Elgars and had a lovely afternoon in the woods.

During part of September we were all away from home and my stepmother had met the Elgars at Hasfield Court, where there was a party for the Gloucester Festival. He took her in to dinner and one of the first things he said was:

'How is my sweet Dorabella?'

'Oh! So it has got to that, has it?' said my stepmother.

'That's a quotation from Mozart's *Così fan tutte,* don't you know it?'

This piece of information was retailed to me in a letter from my stepmother, and a few days afterwards I had a letter from E. E. with the musical quotation from *Così* on the back of the envelope. He wrote:

We missed you at Hasfield very much and I could have made you useful as well as——ah! I didn't write the other word. Well: Caractacus is to be rehearsed at St. James' Hall on Thursday at about eleven and my fate sealed at two o'c. I hope your croquet will be good and that you will have the tea service (it is sure to be that) for your very own, and then some Sunday at Whampton you can give us tea and fire eggs at me as of yore.

Believe me, Amicably

Sept. 24. 1898   EDWARD ELGAR

Ever afterwards I was Dorabella.

I had to think of something to call him, and I hit upon 'Your Excellency' as being what I wanted. I think they liked it; anyway, the Lady always referred to him in her letters to me, and also when she spoke of him, as 'H. E.' from that time on.

Perhaps I should explain that I always spoke of Alice Elgar to E. E. as 'the Lady'.

I first made the acquaintance of Carice Elgar at Forli. She was, at this time, about eight years old and had just gone to Miss Burley's school in Great Malvern. She was a dear little girl, very properly behaved and rather prim, and she did try so hard to keep her father in order! It was rather a strain at meal-times as Carice used to stand behind her chair with an expression of patient disapproval on her face, waiting for silence till she could say Grace. Sometimes she had to wait quite a long time, which was most upsetting.

Unfortunately I have kept very few of the Lady's letters, but I remember quite well one in which she wrote most mysteriously about 'some wonderful and most exciting music, dear Dora! You simply must come soon and hear. I have promised H. E. not to say a word.'[1]

On the first of November there was a Philharmonic Concert at Worcester. I reached the Public Hall in time for most of the rehearsal and sat with the Lady.

Then we went out to luncheon. The composer was in high spirits but I could get nothing out of either of them about the new music. All he said was: 'You wait till we get home. *Japes!*'—taking up a spoon and conducting something with it. And I had to be content with that. After the Concert we all went to tea, as usual, with the Hydes, and at last we arrived home at Forli.

No sooner inside the door than E. E. fled upstairs to the study, two steps at a time—I after him, the Lady following at a more sedate pace.

'Come and listen to this,' and he played me a very odd tune —it was the theme of the *Variations*—and then went on to play sketches, and in some cases completed numbers, of the *Variations* themselves. I turned over and saw the next page headed 'C. A. E.', the Lady's initials, something dedicated to her, evidently. Very serene and lovely—and in some curious way *like* her. Then he turned over two pages and I saw No. III, R. B. T., the initials of a connexion of mine. This *was* amusing! Before he had played many bars I began to laugh, which rather annoyed me. You don't generally laugh when you hear a piece of music for the first time dedicated to someone you know, but I just couldn't help it, and when it was over we both roared with laughter!

---

[1] The Lady used underlining freely in her letters, and those who knew her will understand my use of italics when quoting her spoken words.

'But you've made it *like* him! How on earth have you done it?'

'Go on, turn over.' And the next piece was called No. IV, W. M. B., another connexion and a great friend; very energetic and downright. Why did it remind me of him so?

I think he then played 'Troyte', and a shout of laughter followed.

'What do you think of that for the giddy Ninepin?'

After that, 'Nimrod'.

'That must be a wonderful person, when am I going to meet him?'

A voice from near the fire-place:

'Oh, you *will* like him, he is the *dearest* person.' (As a matter of fact it was more than a year later when I first saw Mr. Jaeger.)

Then I turned over and had a shock. No. X, 'Dorabella.' Being overcome by many emotions I sat silent when it was over.

'Well, how do you like *that*—hey?'

I murmured something about its being charming and rather like a butterfly, but I could think of nothing sensible to say; my mind was in such a whirl of pleasure, pride, and almost shame that he should have written anything so lovely about *me*. The voice from the fire-place came to my rescue:

'Isn't it beautiful, dear Dora? I do *hope* you like it.'

CRAEG LEA

MY first visit to the Elgars at Craeg Lea, Malvern Wells, was in May 1899. They had moved in about two months before and I had heard much about it. It was a better house than Forli, larger and far more comfortable, and the view across the valley of the Severn was perfectly charming. I was never tired of looking at it, with the changing lights and shadows of passing clouds.

Since my last visit to them at Forli, in November, I had been down for the day to another Worcester Philharmonic, in January 1899, and had had three letters from E. E.

Malvern Feb 22

My dear Dorabellllla

How many ells long is that? The Variations are finished & yours is the most cheerful; everybody says it is the 'prettiest'—of course intending to compliment the music not the Variationee—that's you. I hope it may be done soon & then we shall have some curious opinions. I have orchestrated you well.

Yrsever

ED. ELGAR

Malvern Sunday

My dear Dorabella

(Will that do?)

Many thanks for the account of the match—it is so kind of you to invite me to anything good, after its over—are you living backwards like the Queen in Alice?

Oh! the fickleality of you.

It is indiscreet of your co-variant (ahem!) W. M. B. to say you are all to be played by Richter. He, R., is to see 'em in Vienna very soon and—if he is not prevented by certain London——(mystery!) will play you all in the Spring (tra! la!).

You won't be produced at a festival—dear me! child, the vanity of you!

When shall we see any of you again?

14

Craeg Lea

My wife is better
Me   do.
The cook   do.

Yours ever
ED. ELGAR

These dull days (Sundays) the giddy IXpin & Me find nothing to
do but to make Peter (Miss Smart's cat) tipsy & send him home
about 4.30 in an extremely dissipated condition—we propose it but
it hasn't been done yet.

Malvern March 26. 99

My dear Dorabella

How funny you are!

Don't you know yet that 'England' is sufficient address for me??
The idea.

No: I shall not tell: you must find out all about Craeg Lea.

Well: Richter has telegraphed that he will produce the Variations
& I think 'Dorabella' is to be published separately as well (of course)
as in the set: how like you that!

This is a nice house & a gorjus view: when are you coming to
see it: it would be nice to see you again if you don't arrive hot &
tired & cross off a tyre-be-punctured bicycle.

A's at church & so shd. I be but I have an untidy eye wh. I am
trying to mend: perhaps this accounts for my wild penmanship and
then again perhaps it doesn't.

Everyrs
ED. ELG————R

I went down to Worcester on 4 May for another Philharmonic
Concert and, after the usual merry tea-party at 21 Foregate
Street, went back with the Elgars to Malvern and saw Craeg
Lea for the first time. The study was larger than at Forli and,
with its exquisite view, really made the most delightful room.
I am sure it must have been delightful to work in.

That evening E. E. played the whole of the *Variations* and
played the 'Intermezzo'[1] again afterwards for me to dance to;

[1] E. E. said that there was only a trace of the 'Enigma' theme in the 'Intermezzo' which no one would be likely to find unless he knew where to look
for it.

but I would rather have sat still and heard him play it, I should not have cared how often; the thrill of it was still upon me.

'You wait till you hear it properly played by a decent orchestra; that'll make you sit up!'

Looking through the music and counting up how many of the 'Variations' I knew and how many I had only heard of, I remembered how puzzled I had been by seeing 'E. D. U.' over the Finale.

'Who on earth is E. D. U.?' I asked.

'Well, I should have thought you'd know *that*.'

But I was quite stupid and said, 'I don't know any friend of yours whose name begins with "U".'

'It doesn't begin with "U".'

As he put the slightest possible emphasis on 'begin' my wits at last woke up.

'Oh! of course,' I said rather shyly, knowing that 'Edu' was what the Lady called him—and no one else, so far as I knew. 'It's you.'

'That's a secret. Will you remember?'

Next day we spent most of the morning on the British Camp. We told each other stories of the 'Variations' whom I knew, and laughed aloud about two of them in particular: delightful companions with whom we had both of us, on different occasions, had such a good time; whose personalities and even little eccentricities had been so uncannily 'reflected' in the music. We also spent a good deal of time that morning going over the story of Caractacus. Walking along the earthworks we imagined Caractacus and his forces going down the hill-side to their disastrous encounter with the Romans, the forest glade where Orbin met Eigen, and the final betrayal of Caractacus and his family into the hands of the enemy. I need hardly say that the story lost nothing in the telling. The whole scene was quite unforgettable. The glorious view over miles and miles of country, the solitude and aloofness of the place, and above all hearing him tell of what had so recently filled his mind— there, on the very spot, the centre of the story.

That afternoon I went into Great Malvern in the brake[1] and chose photographs to put into my copy of *Caractacus*, which was falling to pieces. I had told E. E. previously, in a letter, that I was going to have *Caractacus* bound, and he had replied with a postcard:

We have awful colds, coffs, sneezes, etc. and are miseries to our-selves & neighbours & hate life. Why bind Caractacus? he was unbound by order of the Czar—Claudius.

In aste   yrs E. E.

That evening I produced the photographs I had bought and mounted ready for the vocal score, and after a good deal of patience and persuasion I induced him to write the title of each under the pictures; but he badly wanted to put 'The British Scamp' (I saw that he had written it on his blotting pad) under the British Camp picture, and then he tried to put it under his own portrait.

Of that evening my diary says: 'IXpin to dinner. Great larks.' And of the next day: 'Breakfast 7.30. Saw His Ex. off at Malvern Wells Sta. 8.15. Did news-cuttings nearly all day. Home at 7.'

During this May visit I also heard a good deal of *Gerontius*. In June I was there again for a day and heard more. I remember thinking and saying, 'What on earth will an ordinary oratorio chorus do with this?' Most vividly do I remember a third visit, 31 July 1899, this time to Birchwood, on a very hot summer day. I had bicycled from Wolverhampton, forty miles, and arrived, rather warm and dusty, at the cart-track leading up through the woods to the house. When I was nearly there I thought I would rest, out of sight, and get cool. I heard the piano in the distance and, not wishing to lose more of it than I need, I soon went on. In a moment I came in sight of the Lady sitting on a fallen tree just below the windows. She had a red parasol. I think

---

[1] A two-horse open vehicle which ran regularly between West Malvern and Great Malvern. The Elgars used to hang out a Union Jack when anyone wished to stop it.

she sat there partly to warn people off—particularly people with bicycles who had been known to commit the awful crime of ringing a bell to announce their arrival. Leaning the bicycle against a tree, I went and sat down by her without speaking. He was playing the opening of Part II, and those who know the music well will understand what it was like to hear that strangely aloof, ethereal music for the first time in such surroundings. Each time I hear it I think of that beautiful place and that glorious day with the sunshine coming through the lace-work of greenery and branches and the deep-blue sky over all.

Soon, however, the music ceased and a voice behind us remarked: 'Are you two going to have your photographs taken, or what?'

That afternoon the Lady said she was busy, and we went into the woods and sat down on the ground. After a bit E. E. said: 'If we are perfectly quiet perhaps someone will come and talk to us.'

In a few minutes a robin came, and then a little love of a fieldmouse. It ran towards us in jerks and came quite close, within touching distance, without a sign of fear. Later on E. E. lay down and went to sleep, and I felt very like dozing, what with the effect of my forty-mile ride, the hum of the bees, and the sheer beauty of it all.

'Tank-y-tank-tank', said the sheep-bell distantly. Lo! it was tea-time.

We went back to the house and had tea, and afterwards he settled down to the piano and I to my usual work of turning over. The music was in manuscript, but 'Praise to the Holiest' was, as far as I remember, nearly completed in vocal score form. He went straight through it, and after the nine bars tied chord passage at the end, he stopped, sat back in his chair and got a pipe out of a pocket. I had been so absorbed, so amazed and overwhelmed by the music that I could say nothing, and there was silence. At last I murmured:

'How perfectly wonderful!' More silence. Then he said:

'How does that strike you?'

What a question! What *could* I say? An idea had come into my mind while he was playing; should I tell him? I summoned up my courage.

'It gives me the impression of great doors opening and shutting.' He turned round in his chair and looked at me.

'Does it? That's exactly what I mean.'

(But it was not until I had heard a really good performance that my 'vision' was realized completely. The impression of an immense crowd of singers in that Region beyond the great doors, and the idea that separate sets of singers added their tributes, like asides to one another—'and in the Garden', 'O generous Love', and in the latter, two groups in conversation, as it were.)

Then we had some of 'Praise to the Holiest' over again and then I asked for the Introduction to Part II which I had heard when I had arrived in the morning. That particular bit of *Gerontius* is inextricably bound up with Birchwood in my mind; every time I hear it the scene comes vividly back to me.

At last I came down to earth and realized with dismay that my time was up and that I had a train to catch at Worcester— and a seven mile bicycle ride. How the time had flown! I collected my things, said good-bye to the Lady and tore myself away. H. E. walked with me to the lane which led down to the main road. It had clouded over and had become very sultry; it was pretty obvious that a storm was coming up.

'I wish you hadn't to go off like this,' he said, looking rather anxiously at the sky; 'come again soon.' I looked back when I got to the bottom of the hill. He was still standing there; I threw up an arm and got an answer. I rode as fast as I could into Worcester, the storm coming up behind me, but I got to the shelter of the station just in time. The first huge drops of rain were falling and the lightning lit up the dark staircase as I carried my bicycle up to the platform. I bought a postcard at the bookstall and wrote three words on it: 'High and Dry'— and posted it, as the train came in, water pouring off it like a cascade. *What* a day! How the music sang in my head all the way home. We out-distanced the storm and left it behind us. I bought an evening paper at Birmingham (my people would have thought it odd if I had not done so), but I found it unopened by my side when I reached my journey's end.

That September it was Worcester's turn for the Three Choirs Festival, and the *Variations* were down for the Wednesday Concert in the Public Hall: the second performance after the production at St. James's Hall, in June, under Richter. There were several of 'us' there and my stepmother came down for it too. As she had three relations—brother, brother-in-law, and stepdaughter—'Variants', and at least three friends besides, it is no wonder she wished to be present. I sat with W. M. B. and I am afraid we did not behave very well; it was not easy to do so sitting next to him as he always saw the fun in everything. He was immensely interested and amused by 'R. B. T.', obviously seeing the likeness but quite at a loss—as we all were at first—to know how the likeness had been contrived. At the end of it he burst out with:

'Well, I'm damned!'

When the Finale was over he remarked: 'Well, you're the best of the bunch anyway!'

He did not understand his own variation, that was clear, nor did the rest of the party. I shall never forget the gauntlet that I had to run afterwards, at the Star Hotel, Worcester, where we were all staying for the Concert. He wanted to know what each variation meant including his own, and I was put in a very awkward position, with my father and stepmother (W. M. B.'s sister) there as I could not possibly have told what I knew about them, they would not have understood.

Then of course they demanded to know what the Intermezzo meant and I suggested—rather lamely—wasn't it rather a charming dance tune? Of course my father rose to that bait at once:

'What did he want to give you a dance tune for?' But everyone said how charming it was and further criticism was stayed.

People are curious; but there was one person in our house-party there that evening who understood, and she and I looked at one another. That was Mrs. W. M. Baker, a lovely amateur singer and pianiste and a most charming friend to me. I was rather on edge that evening, as may be imagined, and she saved me by her understanding and sympathy.

I cannot remember how many other 'Variations' I saw that evening, but I think it was a pretty fair gathering of the clan. It was a splendid performance, and E. E. was right, he *had* orchestrated us well, and No. X was so lovely that I felt—that first time—that I wanted to hide somewhere. My sensations when I hear it now, after more than forty years, are very different. Of all Elgar's music the *Variations* bring back most vividly the memories of those enchanting days and the honour that was mine to be one of that company of fourteen friends.

And now, in 1946, I am the only one left and must bear the honour alone.

But it is as it should be: I was the youngest.

On 1 November 1899, I had a wire from Malvern—'Alice ill can you come.' Fortunately I was able to go and set off next day, arriving at Craeg Lea in the forenoon. I found the poor little Lady looking like nothing on earth and obviously feeling wretchedly ill, but still up and dressed. I did my utmost to get her to bed and succeeded early in the evening, and she was really thankful to be there. As for E. E., he was in high spirits. The *Gerontius* proofs were arriving in batches every few days with voluminous letters from Mr. Jaeger, some of which I had to read aloud while E. E. checked the corrections, with a constant flow of interjections and comments.

'What does he say? The crazy old Moss-head! I'm not going to alter that for him or anyone else.'

On one occasion he got up and fetched a trombone that was standing in a corner and began trying to play passages in the score. He didn't do it very well and often played a note higher or lower than the one he wanted, in fact anywhere but in the 'middle of the note'; and as he swore every time that happened I got into such a state of hysterics that I didn't know what to do. Then he turned on me:

'How *can* you expect me to play this dodgasted thing if you laugh?'

I went out of the room as quickly as I could and sat on the stairs, clinging to the banisters till the pain eased, but it was no good. I couldn't stop there as he went on making comic noises, so I went downstairs out of ear-shot for a bit.

Next day I had little difficulty in keeping the Lady in bed. She said: 'I *do* like hearing you both laugh. Then I know that H. E. is happy and that makes me feel better!'

There were various things the Lady wanted me to do for her in Great Malvern, and when I went in to see her just before starting she asked me to go and find out if there was anything 'dear Edward' wanted. So I tapped at the study door.

'Come in.'

'I'm going into Malvern on some errands for the Lady; is there anything you want?'

'Yes. You. Come in and shut the door.'

'I really can't stop now; I've put the flag out and the brake is almost due—I simply must go.'

'I can't see what is the good of your coming all the way from Wolverhampton if you go and spend half the day in Malvern directly you arrive.'

'You unreasonable thing——Mercy! there's the brake,' and I dashed downstairs and out of the door only just in time. I was lucky in Malvern; I did all the Lady's errands and got back to Craeg Lea in time for luncheon.

That afternoon the Lady had a good sleep. I went out for a short walk with E. E., but we did not wish to be away from the house for long. That evening we had a lot of music, mostly *Gerontius*, Part I, and I did hours of 'turning over', which delighted me.

Then came Saturday and another batch of proofs. E. E. worked hard at them alone and I did things for the Lady and sat with her a good deal. She told me that he had to go up to Leeds on Monday and how *should* she manage his packing? I said I was quite a useful packer and mightn't I do it?

'You can have his portmanteau brought in here, dear Dora, and I could tell you just what to put in. Would you do that?' So that was settled and it made her quite happy.

That evening the proofs, which were nearly ready to be returned, were put on one side and E. E. settled down to the piano. I think we had the *Sea Pictures* all through and sketches and bits of *Cockaigne* as well. Then he went back to the *Variations*, and I asked about the 'Enigma' and what *was* the tune that 'goes and is not played'?

'Oh, I shan't tell you that, you must find it out for yourself.'

'But I've thought and racked my brains over and over again.'

'Well, I'm surprised. I thought that you, of all people, would guess it.'

'Why "me of all people"?'

'That's asking questions!'

On another occasion I asked him again and he said:

'Haven't you guessed it *yet*? Try again.' In fact, he egged me on to go on thinking till I got it, and I really believe he would have been pleased and amused if I had done so. But as years passed I came to have the feeling that he did not want the solution found, and as time still further went on and no one guessed it he determined never to divulge it himself. He always changed the subject at once if anyone began it. I believe that the only two people who shared his confidence were the Lady and Mr. Jaeger.

Then we moved over to the fire and began talking about some of the *Variations* and how splendid they sounded on the orchestra.

'Why, I haven't seen you since Worcester! Didn't they play well? I saw you sitting next W. M. B.; how did he like it? Do tell me what he said.'

And so we went on and on, E. E. standing with his back to

the fire and I sitting in a big arm-chair. Suddenly he took me by my two hands and half lifted me up:

'And how did you like *yourself*, my Dorabella?'

Then I tried to tell him how wonderful I thought it, and how it was far too delicate and lovely for the likes of me.

'Well of course it is! We all know that.'

But I wouldn't be put off and I said how marvellous it was to feel oneself part of the music which had been acclaimed by half the world as being his greatest work.

'You dear child,' he said, and kissed me on the forehead.

Monday morning arrived and I thought the Lady much better. The packing was duly done and the clothes that E. E. was to change into were put ready. I ordered his cab. He was playing Bach Fugues when I went in to say that everything was ready, and would he go and change?

'I'm not going: I'm going to stop at home.'

I stood doubtfully by the door.

'Oh, very well; but you can bring my things in here, I'll change by the fire.'

I brought them in and departed. The piano ceased for about three minutes and then began again, so, wondering what was happening, and getting anxious about the time, I ventured in. Bach was going on louder than ever and E. E. was sitting at the piano in a clean shirt, and trousers.

'You can just do some work and dress me. I'm not going to stop playing.'

How I got him dressed I don't know. I laughed so much I could hardly fasten anything; collar-studs or tie. Yes, *tie as well*; and I made quite a good job of it too. I went and told the Lady how naughty he'd been and I was really afraid she would laugh more than was good for her. Mary, their very nice maid, came upstairs to tell us that the cab was at the door and she took down the luggage. I ran along to the study to tell E. E. Goodbyes were said and, at last, Mary and I saw him off. At tea-time the Lady was so much better that she came into the study and sat by the fire and we did newspaper cuttings all the evening.

I went home next day, and had a letter from E. E. the morning after thanking me for the care of 'our poor invalid' and saying she was much better.

In January 1900 he came to Wolverhampton for another football match, and in the following May I went down for a Worcester Philharmonic Concert—and at last met 'Nimrod'. After the concert we had a most hilarious tea at the Hydes, and when tea was over we said our farewells and went to Foregate Street station on our way back to Malvern. Mr. Jaeger and I became fast friends at once. He *was* a most delightful person. His English was fluent, not to say voluble, but with a strong German accent. He asked me if I knew Gilbert and Sullivan well and we sang 'Oh, Captain Shaw!' on Foregate Street platform while waiting for the train. E. E. in the background remarked, 'Now they're off.'

That journey was one of the noisiest I have ever made. Our party filled a compartment, and all the way Mr. Jaeger was telling me with great volubility and much gesture how wonderful *Gerontius* was. E. E. was trying to stop him and was calling him a whole string of comic names, and the rest of the party were in fits of laughter.

On Sunday E. E. and Mr. Jaeger shut themselves into the study all the morning. When I came back from church, having called for Carice at her school on the way, I found them still busy. The Ninepin came to luncheon and it was all most amusing. When they came into the dining-room E. E. saw Carice, standing behind her chair, waiting.

'Hullo, Fishface! Quite well?'

'Yes thank you, father.'

' "Yes thank you, father," ' imitated E. E. in a high sort of squeak; after which the unfortunate child was expected to say Grace!

When E. E. was at the top of his form meals used to be

exciting. He kept up a running fire of absurd remarks, comments, chaff, and repartee. I often laughed so much that I could hardly eat and was positively afraid to drink. Also it did not help matters to have the Lady, at the bottom of the table—not always completely approving, particularly if Carice was present —putting in remarks to try to check the flow:

'Oh, Edward dear, how *can* you?' or 'Oh, Edward, *really*!'

'Cheer up, Chicky!' was all she got for her pains.

On this occasion I think the fun was even more than usually fast and furious, because Mr. Jaeger was there and E. E. was in the best of good spirits. The climax came when E. E. started conducting with a carving-knife!

But this pitch of excitement and nonsense was never kept up for very long. One of the interesting things about E. E. was his varying moods. I am sensitive to 'atmosphere' and I quickly attuned myself to the mood of the moment and fell in with it. I think that was one of the reasons why we got on so well. There were times when he was quiet and disinclined to talk and as I felt sure that his head was full of music I used to keep perfectly still and not make a sound for fear of disturbing. I used to hope he would go to the piano and play but he seldom did; instead, he wrote something on a piece of music paper. If he went on writing I used to slip out of the room and leave him to it.

Then there were days when he longed for the open air and we spent hours out on bicycles or walking on the Hills or sitting in the woods or by the river. Then he would tell me all sorts of interesting and amusing things—how *silly* it is not to be able to remember any of it! I ought to have written down everything I could remember each evening. Any keeper of a real, proper diary would have. But it never occurred to me to do so. I can only remember that the walks and rambles were a sheer delight. His witty and unexpected comments on things were a never-ending source of amusement, and, when he was feeling like it, he was funny beyond words.

Then there were the rarer occasions when he was frankly

miserable and dispirited and bored. People had been provoking and things had been tiresome. One such occasion is recorded elsewhere. It was the old tale—'. . . sick and tired of mouldy music. I shall give it all up!' He longed for sympathy and distraction from worry. It needed a good deal of tact and care to think of the right things to say or the right line to take; particularly when one found that a person who had been lauded to the skies on a former visit was now flung to earth—though seldom by *him*—but I managed gradually to evolve where the trouble lay and the rest followed more easily. It was most interesting to find that as the minutes went by the mood and misery was giving way and that we should soon be out of the shadows into the sunshine—'Come on, let's do some music!'

But to return to Mr. Jaeger and the day he lunched at Craeg Lea.

Unfortunately he had to go back to London that evening; he told me a great deal about his work and promised to send me a copy of his Analysis of Coleridge-Taylor's *Hiawatha* which was going through the press just then and in which he was immensely interested.

In the years to come he was very good to me and was a most delightful and interesting friend. He sent me a copy of nearly everything of the sort that he wrote. Some of his letters— brimful of interest, dealing with E. E.'s works as they came to be written—were a perfect delight to me. I kept them all till 1914 and then, alas! in a fit of tidying and re-arrangement, I tore up and burned a huge packet of them. How deeply I regret it now! He sent me several proof-copies of E. E.'s works with the strictest injunction to secrecy. Of course I loved having them and prized them tremendously, but I always hoped most fervently that he would not get into trouble for sending them, perhaps depriving some Important Person of the copy which I hugged to myself at a first performance.

I went with him to a great many orchestral concerts, which was not only extremely enjoyable, but was quite a musical education. What I enjoyed most of all was when he took me to a rehearsal in the morning, followed by luncheon at some restaurant, and the concert in the afternoon. That I usually came armed with miniature full scores seemed to please him very much. He used to say:

'Ha! Very good. That is the way to enjoy the music.'

But there were many times when he wrote and asked me to go up for a concert, and when I had said I was uncertain if I could manage it—much as I should like it—he wrote back:

'Now, Dorabella, naughty girl, you must not tease small Germans so!'

It was on one of the first occasions when I met Mr. Jaeger in London—at a rehearsal of the *Variations*, I think—that I tackled him about the Enigma.

'Now, Dorabella, you must be a good girl and not ask me about that. I do not suppose that I could keep it from you if you were to plead with me, but the dear E. E. did make me promise not to tell you.'

'Oh, he did, did he?' I said slowly, 'then I will never ask you.'

He kissed my hand.

'Forgive my funny little foreign ways, Dorabella dear?'

I never mentioned the subject to him again. In those early days I always hoped I might guess the secret myself, and the recollection of this little scene with Nimrod seems far more momentous to me now than it did at the time.

The first few letters that I had from Mr. Jaeger were full of comments on *Gerontius* as the proofs came through.

May 25th, 1900. Gerontius grows more & more masterly as it proceeds. It is quite wonderful in parts: mystic, sublime, superb. I have to write a preliminary review of the work in the Musical Times for October, so I am already studying it hard, in Buses, Trains, everywhere. Have it always in my pocket, in fact & go to Bed with it.

We are now discussing the publication of a new pianists arrangement of 'Dorabella' separately and I hope something will come of it. I shall harp on the subject till I have found a good pianist-arranger to make the proper (difficult) P—F arrangement, and till I see the thing in print with a portrait of the original 'Dorabella'. Eh? Fine idea! Send your photo at once!!

June 2nd, 1900.   Dear Miss $\begin{cases} \text{Allegretto } (\stackrel{\downarrow}{=}80) \\ \text{G Major} = \frac{3}{4} \end{cases}$

. . . In Gerontius we have a great, deep <u>thinker</u> & <u>dreamer</u> allying wonderful music to wonderful words, a powerful intellect doing its greatest for a great poem. . . . There is stuff in Gerontius that is perfectly beautiful, original & heart rending!

June 9th, 1900.   Dear friend of E. E.   He has arrived
. . . and is going to the Götterdämmerung tonight & the Richter Concert on Monday. Why cometh No. X of Variations Op 27 not to that? . . . E. E. has sent the completion of his blessed Gerontius. The work undoes me utterly if I am in the mood. A few friends are coming to my House tomorrow to hear some of it. Elgar, whom I saw half an hour ago, says that <u>perhaps</u> he will come too. The Chorus Parts will not be in the hands of the B'ham Singers for another 3 weeks or more; so your honoured aunt[1] must possess her soul in Patience. I'll send you an advance copy of the Vocal Score for your <u>very</u> <u>private</u> use (mind you: Private!!) as soon as I possibly can. But that will not be for a week or two or three.

. . . No, the majority of the B'ham audience will not be able to appreciate Gerontius first time; too subtle & original & too mystic & beautiful, but a few like yourself & others will wax 'Wild' with enthusiasm.

September 29th, 1900. In a few days I will give myself the pleasure of sending you a copy of my wretched analysis. I hope your Ladyship will deign to consider it not unworthy of His Excellency's magnum bonum, I mean opus. (though it <u>is</u> bonum— in fact 'optime'). Mr. Johnstone the chairman of the Committee (B'ham) told me yesterday that Richter likes the work as much as I do! If that's so he must indeed think much of it. I am going to the <u>whole</u> of the Festival chaperoning a German musician, Professor Buths, of Düsseldorf, my native town. I hope to see you there after all.

[1] Mrs. Hodgson: a member of the Birmingham Festival Chorus for many years.

On 19 July 1900, I went down to Birchwood late in the afternoon, taking my bicycle to Worcester by train and riding out from there. It was very hot. I got to the house at about 7 o'clock but found no one at home. They had warned me that they might be late getting back and that if I got there first I was to make myself at home. I had unpacked, and helped to lay the table for supper before they came in sight and I played the game of acting hostess to them. E. E. had been in Birmingham all day and was pretty tired; the Lady had been shopping in Malvern and they were laden with parcels.

After supper E. E. and I went out of doors. I wanted to stay and help the Lady but she would not hear of it. 'I can manage quite well, thank you, dear Dora. Do go out with Edward; it will be lovely and cool out there.' Nothing loath, of course I went. It was so lovely being able to step straight out of the house, across the tiniest of gardens, into the woods, and there was a delicious spot where one came to the edge of the ridge on which Birchwood stands and could sit down on the slope and see the view of the Malvern Hills and the Severn Valley stretched out before one between the tree trunks. We sat there a long while that evening and then we went to see the glow-worms. They *were* a sight! There was a bank with ever so many on it shining most wonderfully. He lectured me on them—how they made the light and what it was for: the females to attract a male and the males to warn off enemies.

The woods in the moonlight were most attractive, but I do not think I should ever have ventured there alone! The silence —one hardly dared tread for fear of the snap of a twig under foot—the dense black shadows of the tree trunks and the queer shapes that things take on in moonlight, and strange little eerie noises. And then a white owl looking for a supper, flew past, close by us, without a sound.

'Don't jump like that—you'll frighten everyone.' 'What about me being frightened?' He laughed. 'You ridic'lous child! It's getting late. Let's go in and do some music.'

At all times of day those woods were lovely. There were no

made paths but it was easy walking in dry weather as there was no undergrowth. The wild flowers were a joy—and the birds! Very early next morning I hung out of my little bedroom window and sniffed the exquisite scents—Debussy's *Les parfums de la Nuit* always reminds me of it.

Then of course the whole scene is wrapped up with the music that I heard, chiefly *Gerontius*; every available interval was filled with it.

After breakfast there was a thunderstorm. I was busy turning over for E. E. and the storm was getting rather close and I did not like it. I remember how the lightning shone on the music paper, sometimes blue and sometimes pink, and at last a hot white light and a crash of thunder both at once. The noise was too great for piano playing so we stopped and did other things. I remember being supremely thankful.

The weather cleared after luncheon but was very steamy and close. My diary says: 'The woods were like a watered greenhouse, but we found a dry place and worked there all the afternoon correcting proofs.'

It was cooler next day; I did all sorts of jobs to help the Lady, turned over for a lot more music and departed on my bicycle for Worcester and home after an early tea. What a delicious time it had been!

It was terribly difficult to return to normal life and occupations after one of those visits. Of course I had to tell my people something of what I had heard and done but one had to be very careful. They demanded that I should sit down and play 'bits' of *Gerontius* to them. I could have done so but I dreaded giving wrong impressions, so I usually got out of it somehow. People who thought themselves musical in those days had the oddest ideas. When I played and sang a bit of 'Praise to the Holiest' my father said:

'But *surely* he's going to use the fine tune in Ancient and Modern? He'll be making a terrible mistake if he doesn't.'

There was no more playing 'bits of *Gerontius*' after that.

I found, however, that my father was by no means alone in

thinking that Elgar should use a well-known hymn tune in this way. People of his age, brought up in the Bach and Handel tradition, were accustomed to this idea and expected it. To my great surprise I found, many years later, that my father-in-law —a gifted amateur musician—thought, and said, exactly the same thing.

Then at last came the Birmingham Festival, and Wednesday, 3 October saw the production of *Gerontius*. My diary says:
'Too wonderful and clever to describe here, but performance not good.'
I remember well wondering what to put. The performance lacked so much of what one knew was there. The chorus had not had enough time to learn their music: the Elgar idiom was like a foreign tongue that cannot be mastered in a few weeks. To crown all, a soloist began one of his 'pieces' a semitone flat—or was it sharp?—*and stuck to it*—(bless his heart!) He was so upset about it afterwards. It was all rather dreadful and I felt afterwards that I wanted to get home quickly and meet nobody. The poor Elgars had escaped back to their hotel and saw no one—how my heart ached for him and what he must have felt that day!
On 15 October came a letter from Nimrod which I quote almost in full.

October 14th, 1900. I have been 'pitched into' for being enthusiastic over Gerontius. I don't mind a bit. It was lack of enthusiasm both in the performers & amongst the critics which riled me at B'ham & afterwards, when I read the critiques. Now you Englishers have a composer at last you might be excused if you waxed enthusiastic over him for once in a way. But oh dear no! If this were only a wretched new opera or a dull new oratorio by Mascagni or Perosi, the papers would have had columns of gossip & gush about those 2 frauds. But its only an English musician (not an actress or a jockey or a Batsman) and he is treated like a very ordinary nobody. Oh you unpatriotic creatures. I won't say a word about the performance, but I suffered purgatory!! this disenchantment after my hours of exaltation & refreshment at the Pianoforte was too cruel. I was of course unfortunately placed in a way, for the music was so very familiar to me that I concentrated all my attention on the actual performance, never glancing at the score or analysis, Old St—— the choir-mess-ter ought to be boiled & served on Toast for having had us in Purgatory for nigh 2 Hours. . . .

You ought to come to Düsseldorf (my native place) & attend a Festival (under Buths) to get an idea of an ideal Hall for such a gathering. Such ample corridors, cloakrooms, Restaurants; and a big lovely garden (with al fresco refreshments) all round the Hall!

All the Germans I spoke to at B'ham (Richter, Dr. Otto Lessman, Prof. Buths, etc. etc.) were enthusiastic about Elgar's work. Directly it was over Buths grasped my hand (coram publico) & blurted out: 'Ein wunderbares Werk; eins der schönsten Werke die ich kenne' etc. etc. . . . To be with Buths for a whole week continuously (except Bedtime) exhausted me, & I longed for a chat with a woman. And it was a fruitless longing. So I say: Where was my co-variation? In Print No. 9 & 10 'were not divided'. Then why in festive Brummagem? I never forgive you that! . . .

Dear E. E. sent me quite a depressing letter last week. I told him it was weak & wicked to write like that. So he replied at once in a better strain. I told him to look at the Introduction & first Allegro of Beethoven's 'Pathétique' (Sonata). That is the mood in which to look adverse circumstances in the face & defy them.

Kindest regards.

Yours sincerely
NIMROD-JAEGER

On 22 November 1900, Edward Elgar received the degree of Mus.D. of Cambridge.

During that winter I had six letters from Mr. Jaeger, parts of which I quote.

December 27th, 1900. I'm still trying hard to get Gerontius performed in London, but it is almost hopeless. I still hope Wood will do it. . . .

Yours sincerely
A. J. JAEGER

January 20th, 1901. I think E. is also finishing that Symphony at last. He had the BLUES terribly about 3 weeks ago, but last time he wrote he was joyful.

'Gosh man, I've got a tune in my head' he wrote to me.

January 28th, 1901. [Postcard] Greeting! Variations, not omitting Intermezzo, at Düsseldorf under Prof. Buths on Feb. 7th. I do wish you could go over. Am urging the Dr. to go & hear first performance in Germany. Nice place D'dorf!

NIMROD

February 18th, 1901. Dear Dorabella. Your dear Doctor E. E. is in town & this morning we went together to Queen's Hall to hear Wood conduct the Gerontius Prelude & Angel's Farewell (Kirkby Lunn as the 'Angel'). Oh, Dorabella, the stuff sounded most beautiful, most moving, most elevating. It is the highest thing in English art (musical art) & honestly, I say again it seems to me the noblest, aloofest thing since Parsifal. Wood conducted it with loving care; spent 1½ hours on it & the result was a performance which completely put Richter's into the Shade. I was deeply affected & I felt more than I could express to dear E. E.

April 15th, 1901. By the way, Wood has placed the Elgar Variations in the London Festival Programme. He has just written to me 'How beautiful the Variations are!' At last! Brewer tells me he wants to do them at the Gloucester Festival (Shire Hall). 'We' are getting on, n'est ce pas? . . . The Dr. has just written me a letter in his most Elgaresque style; insults me by saying he would like ½ hour with me, to talk some sense into that German Vacuum! etc. etc. He is a 'killing' person.

April 28th, 1901. Dear Dorabella, I went to the rehearsal on Friday morning and again yesterday when E. E. turned up, and I can assure you Wood makes these things (Variations) hum. I have never heard anything more daringly, devilishly brilliant & boisterous than Troyte or G. R. S., more gorgeous in colour than 'Nimrod', more dainty & graceful than the lovely 'Dorabella'. I sat next M. Colonne all the time yesterday. He dropped in for a few minutes, but he was at once interested & stayed all the time. He was most appreciative, and from being merely interested & saying 'c'est difficile' & 'c'est charmant' he grew warmer & warmer in his praise & more & more astonished, till 'Nimrod' drew from him an enthusiastic 'Ah' & the remark 'it is the best & very beautiful' (He speaks little English) & Dorabella delighted him immensely. 'C'est vraiment delicieux' & similar expressions came from him & at the end (Wood played that stunning coda superbly) he was quite enthusiastic. When Elgar came down from the platform, C took E's right hand in both his own & made him quite a long speech of congratulation. Elgar was quite touched. The orchestra gave him (E) a splendid ovation, I never heard a better one at any rehearsal.

On 9 May 1901, I went down for the Worcester Philharmonic's performance of *Gerontius*.[1] They did it splendidly and one heard it properly at last. It was not, of course, a complete performance. The Chorus was not large enough for the 'Demons' in Part II, so the whole of that was omitted; but it was a joy to hear most of the work sung as the composer wished it. William Green was the Gerontius and I remember how beautifully he sang. Hélène Valma sang the Angel music and she also sang the *Sea Pictures*. We all went to tea at the Hydes'. My diary says: 'Drove up all together from Gt. M. Station, Dr. E. very mad!'

'10th May. Friday. Did cuttings most of the day. William Green is very nice. He stayed till 3. The L. and I drove into Gt. M. with him and came back in the brake.'

When we returned E. E. heard us and called out to me: 'Child, come up here. I've got a tune that will knock 'em— knock 'em flat,' and he played the Military March No. 1 in D. I *was* thrilled; the whole thing carried one along so splendidly —and as to the coda, I thought it glorious.

'Military March in D this is. What note does it begin on?'
'E flat.'
'Yah! there's a joke! Talk of jokes—what about the trombones here'—pointing to a passage—'they'll have some fun!'

My diary for that day finishes: 'Had a nice evening. Heard *Cockaigne, and* the Quick Marches for Military Band—Oh! my *Goodness*!'

---

[1] Part I and selections from Part II.

35

I think nowadays orchestras and bands spoil the March in D utterly by beginning it too fast and taking the Trio much too slow. E. E. played it through that evening in almost strict quick-march time, making very little of the 'Largamente'. Moreover, as it is usually played now, the inner parts of the first section have very little chance.

Unfortunately there is no mention in my diary of another occasion of exuberance and laughter four years later when I first heard the No. 4 March in G. The drum part—so far as I can remember—was the peak of the triumph. The composer *was* pleased with it, and I am not surprised.

E. E. came in to dinner that evening in a bright red golf blazer with brass buttons, over his evening shirt.

'I say, you *are* smart,' I remarked admiringly.

'Well, if W. M. B. wears a pink coat at dinner why shouldn't I wear this?'

'He only wears a pink coat on state occasions when he has grand people to dinner, like you; when I'm there he wears an old Ledbury Hunt coat which I like better; it's quieter!'

'Well, I'm not quiet. Far from it.'

I pretended to look under the table.

'It's no use looking. You won't see satin knee-breeches and silk stockings!'

After dinner that evening we had a lot more music and I heard *Cockaigne* for the first time. It *was* a riot! The noise we made!—and I think the Lady really enjoyed it, she literally sobbed with laughter.

The ingenious way in which the Military Band is heard first of all from afar and then it comes crashing round the corner— in the middle of its tune. And then of course there is the priceless other band heard in the offing. I remember being just a little shocked at the impish way in which the composer has suggested a Salvation Army Band apparently searching for the desired key!

The average Cockney has a large fund of rather sardonic

EDWARD ELGAR AND A. J. JAEGER

At Hasfield Court, Gloucester. September 1901

humour and this trait is most faithfully reproduced by Elgar in *Cockaigne*.

For Saturday, 11 May, my diary says: 'Cuttings again. Miss Norbury to Luncheon & the Ninepin. Went home 4.20. His Ex. played golf with Mr. Jones but knocked off on purpose to see me off at Malvern Wells. There's a dear for you!'

I do not think I went to Malvern all that summer. The Three Choirs Festival was at Gloucester that year, but I did did not go. My people went to stay with Mr. and Mrs. W. M. Baker at Hasfield Court where there was a large house-party for the Festival. The Elgars were there and also Mr. Jaeger. I had letters from both afterwards asking where *I* was. A friend in the party sent me a photograph—not a very good one —of E. E. taking photographs by the porch at Hasfield. He had evidently just taken one of Mr. Jaeger after a bout of single-sticks with one of the Baker boys.

Round about the year 1900 the three boys had woven themselves into a romantic atmosphere engendered by a study of Royalist plots, taking the characters of Prince Rupert, the Duke of Buckingham, and the Earl of Rochester.

When the Elgars visited Hasfield soon after the inception of this idea, Elgar of course entered heart and soul into the whole business, becoming, oddly enough, 'Nanty Ewart', the rather disreputable Captain of the Brig 'Jumping Jenny', from *Redgauntlet*, which the boys had just been reading. Discrepancy in dates led Elgar to say that he was never quite sure what century he was living in! But this did not in any way prevent the whole affair from flourishing most remarkably. Elgar was always known in the Hasfield circle as 'Nanty', and still is to this day.

The gardens at Hasfield Court provided an attractive *mise-en-scène* for this romantic idea, with lawns sloping down to the long pool, and the dark mysterious paths among the trees.

Considerable correspondence has been preserved and from many letters I have selected one for reproduction.

I had two letters from E. E. in October, one from Leeds (here reproduced) and one a fortnight later from Liverpool. The second, dated 25 October 1901, runs:

My dear Dorabella

I can't help telling you that the fiftieth person has this morning written (since Leeds—I mean) to know who D——a is & how charming she must be.

It is so long since I saw you that I forget if you really are nice or if somebody only imagined you to be. So you must come and tell us.

Whether you are as nice as

or only as unideal as

Eh? No. Perhaps??

One of the things that always fascinated me in the Craeg Lea study was a collection of books bound in green linen which were piled on a shelf of a tall 'what-not' close to the piano. As soon as I could, after arriving on a visit (making sure that wandering around looking at things did not disturb), I used to gravitate towards that shelf and turn over the green books. He wrote, generally in blue pencil on the cover, the name of what was inside. I remember seeing one fat book with 'Symphony' on it, and I said:

'Are you writing a Symphony; How perfectly splendid! Couldn't you possibly play some of it?'

'Possibly.'

In this way I heard much; odds and ends; bits and scraps; and sometimes a good deal more. It was fascinatingly interesting—I can think of no better combination of words for it.

Right Nantz (original flask)
circa: 1744.

Worships (3)

The undersigned,
being humble recipient
of august instructions,
hiccougheth acknow-
ledgment thereof.

signed

X
Nantz Coot
his mark.

onboard
Funbysse Jennye.

MIDLAND RAILWAY
Hotels & Refreshment Rooms.
WILLIAM TOWLE, MANAGER.

TELEGRAPHIC ADDRESS TO ALL
MIDLAND RAILWAY HOTELS.
"MIDOTEL."

MIDLAND RAILWAY
HOTELS.

MIDLAND GRAND.
LONDON.
QUEENS, LEEDS.
ADELPHI, LIVERPOOL.
MIDLAND, BRADFORD.
MIDLAND, DERBY.
MIDLAND, MORECAMBE.
HEYSHAM TOWER.
Nᴿ MORECAMBE.

Queen's Hotel.

Leeds,

Oct 15 1901 190

My dear

I quite hoped you
cd. have come then

think we are

fought players find

quite well — You

prosperously ought t

 for let you come.

Tell 'em so from them, yours to several other people

Affectionate friend

(more so to 

than anybody)

mesto

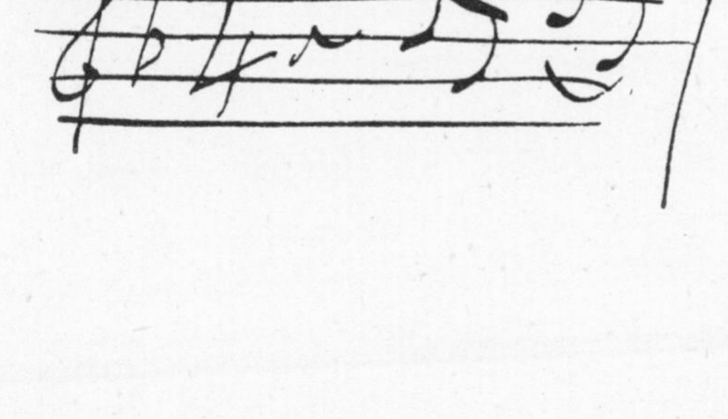

I have often crept back into the study when no one was about, found a page I wanted, and 'made out' (his writing was not easy) some bit of melody that I wished to remember.

With my head singing with 'tunes' it was very trying to be tackled by friends discussing (and running down) *Gerontius* after that awful first performance.

'There simply isn't a real tune in the whole thing—now is there?'

I tried to say that *Gerontius* was packed with tunes one on top of another.

'Well, sing one of them.'

Of course I sang 'Praise to the Holiest'.

'Oh, well, naturally you take the only possible one.'

Then I sang 'Sanctus fortis'.

'Call that a tune? I don't.'

To do justice I must say that those very people have, in time, come to describe *Gerontius* as 'very fine', and one does not bully them by asking them what they mean. That they have gone to hear it a second and even a third time is good enough. They did not know what to say after the first hearing, and who is to blame them?

I did not see the Elgars again in 1901 until 5 December when I went down to Malvern for three days. I found E. E. very busy with the 'book' of *The Apostles*. The study seemed to be full of Bibles. He had a Bible open on the table in front of him and there seemed to be a Bible on every chair and even one on the floor.

'Goodness!' I said. 'What a collection of Bibles! What have you got there besides the Authorized and Revised Versions?'

'I don't know; they've been lent to me. I say, d'you know that the Bible is a most wonderfully interesting book?'

'Yes,' I said, 'I know it is.'

'What do you know about it? Oh, I forgot, perhaps you *do*

know something about it. Anyway, I've been reading a lot of it lately and have been quite absorbed.'

He appeared to be looking out texts and I offered to help.

'I want something that will fit in here'—pointing to a line.

I thought for a moment and fortunately something suitable occurred to me and I quoted it.

'You don't mean to tell me that comes in the Bible? Show it to me.'

I found the eighty-fifth Psalm in one of the Bibles and laid it before him.

'Well! That's extraordinary! It's just what I want here.'

I think it very astonishing, when one looks at the words which are set in *The Apostles* and sees the immense skill with which they have been selected and put together, that the work was mainly done by one who was finding out the beauties of the Bible almost for the first time. Is there anything more moving, for instance, than the words, and music, of that final chorus?

During that visit I heard a lot of sketches and some of the finished numbers of *The Apostles*—and how I loved the whole of the 'Sepulchre' music, with the beautiful Alleluias! We used to work at the words in the day-time mostly and have the music in the evening. But it was on a lovely sunny day when I first heard the Alleluias. I remember standing by the piano, half facing the window with its glorious view across the Severn Valley. One had to be careful, turning over, as some of the pages were loose. The beauty of the music took hold of me and I could hardly see for tears. I was late once, but he knew quite well why and said nothing until the end of the section.

'Do you like that? I thought you would.'

The Lady had begun to use a typewriter, and as the various pages were finished she would take them away downstairs and type them—she said her slow typing would be very disturbing to us! Her typing was not only slow at that time, dear thing! but rather inaccurate as well.

I was copying out something for him at a table in the window and was conscious that she had been in and gone away again, but I had not looked up. Presently he said very quietly:

'Dorabella; come here.'

He pointed to a page. The words were from St. John's Gospel—very solemn and sacred—in question and answer. The Lady had ended each question with a £ instead of a question-mark. It was so dreadful and yet so funny that we were both speechless. A few minutes later the Lady came back with another page.

'Look, Chicky, what you've put here'—and he handed her the sheet.

She looked at it and then sat down rather suddenly on the arm of a chair, and the paper fluttered to the floor. Covering her eyes with one hand she felt for a handkerchief.

At the end of this December visit I became the proud possessor of a title! Its history is as follows.

It was during my visit to the Elgars in May 1899, shortly after their move to Craeg Lea, Malvern Wells, that I first saw the Lady struggling with the classification of press notices. She usually wrote at a heavy table with carved sides, one of a number of Indian pieces from her home at Redmarley. This table was a bit high for a writing-table, and she seemed to prefer rather a low chair. As the table was usually covered with letters and papers, almost hiding a large bound blotting-book, she used sometimes to write nearly shoulder high; but this curious position seemed to suit her.

Imagine her sitting thus, with a large news-cutting book open on the top of everything, and piles of newspapers, some whole and some in long strips, programmes, and open letters littered about on all sides.

On the morning after I arrived I found her deep in this work, scissors in hand, and on the floor by her side an overflowing rubbish-basket.

'Are these the *Caractacus* notices? *Do* let me help.'

'Oh, dear Dora, it would be so *delightful* if you could. *Caractacus* and *Olaf* and all sorts of things, and it *does* take up so much time!'

So that was the beginning, and every time I stayed with them I put in as much time at it as I could. However, there was often so much music to be heard and so much 'turning over' to be done and always some one to be amused, that one had not a great deal of time to spare.

'Hullo! *There* you are. Leave all that mouldy rubbish and come out here with me,' or, 'What on earth are you doing down here? Why can't you come upstairs and talk to me like a decent Christian?'

The news-cutting business was a bit of a trial to the Lady, I think; she felt that it ought to be done, but she made rather heavy weather of it. I was at work one day and she came in with a large, bulging envelope.

'Oh, dear Dora, I am *so* sorry, but you ought to have had these *long* ago. What *will* you do about it?'

Possibly an interleaving job was less effort to me than to her, but she was quite extravagantly pleased and complimentary at the result. As time passed the work was left to me altogether and I just went on with it as a matter of course every time I stayed there. Finally, in December 1901, after a three-day visit, the Lady suggested that I should take the entire work off her hands and take the book, envelopes of cuttings, and everything home with me and do it there.

Such fun we had over the idea, at luncheon!

'You'll want a truck to take it all away in: much better make a bonfire of it in the garden—pity Guy Fawkes' Day's over.'

'Oh, Edward dear, how *can* you be so dreadful? Dear Dora, *don't* attend to him.'

'You'll have to get an extra rubbish-basket.'

'Certainly,' I said, 'I shall get a washing-basket with a handle at each end.'

'Yes, pitch the whole lot in: it will make a nice bed for your cat.'

But all this nonsense about anything as important—not to say sacred—as the Archives was more than the dear Lady could stand, and she said, *sotto voce*:

'You won't throw away *too* much, will you, dear Dora?'

So I became, from that day, Keeper of the Archives; and I well and truly kept them for nearly fifteen years.

It was tremendously interesting work and I loved it. It was very exciting getting all the accounts of the various productions and performances (the Lady sent them to me in great envelopes or parcels), reading them through, and deciding which was the best for putting in the place of honour. It was most interesting to read what the different critics thought and the effect that the music had on them. It always amused me to get a bad notice (a rare event), and I usually gave it a prominent place. Specially amusing was it when the writer thought better of it at a later date and hedged.

It used to be rather amusing, too, when I took a finished volume 'home' and left it there in the shelf with the rest. The Lady, dear little person, was so delighted and so interested and would turn the pages over with almost childish pleasure, admiring the arrangement of programmes and pictures with their gay spots of colour brightening the dull newspaper columns. E. E. never looked at it—in my presence at any rate—he just said something disparaging.

'Goodness, what a waste of time! Why, you might have been here all those hours attending to me!'

I was sitting on the floor in the study one morning, sorting libretto typescript, when the Lady came in with an open letter in her hand.

'Dear darling, do you think you could write a little letter to that *nice* Mr. Smith?'

43

'No, I'm sure I couldn't, Chicky. Have you got page 9, Dorabella?'

'But you simply *must* answer this—nice *kind* little man, he wrote last week.'

'I know he did, bl—— bother him. Well, I can't do it now, I'm busy. I say, can't you find page 9?'

'Yes, but, sweet darling, I'm just going into Malvern and I could catch the early post and then he'd have it to-morrow morning.'

'Well, he's not going to. (*Pause.*) Oh, *don't* stand there, Chicky, looking like a stony image! Give me a piece of paper —not that sort, it's too large. Well, what am I to say to him? Dear Mr. Smith—blast this pen——'

'Oh, Edu darling—*please*——'

At this point, though half-blind with laughter, I found the missing page 9 and, putting it on the table as I passed, slipped out of the room. As I shut the door I heard him say:

'What's Dorabella crying for?'

It was not always that I found E. E. in high spirits when I went to stay with them. In the years between 1897 and 1912 I went so often, first to Malvern and then to Hereford, that such a thing could not be expected.

'I see you've got a letter from Al. What does she say?' my stepmother used to ask.

'They don't sound very grand. He's low in his mind about something and she seems worried to death. They'd rather like it if I could go down.'

And if I could possibly fix my plans I went.

I was a good deal taken up with both parish and town activities at Wolverhampton in those days; helping with entertainments, sales, and bazaars, and attending countless committee meetings. Besides this I ran my own string orchestra for about four years, and I sang in the Wolverhampton Choral Society, under the conductorship of Henry J. Wood, Granville Bantock, and others, every season for eighteen years. E. E.

used to chaff me about the Choral Society, and if I made any sort of criticism he would say:

'What do you know about it? You're only a Chorus Girl!'

Arriving at the Elgars after receiving such a letter I found the little Lady looking rather white and tired.

'Oh, *dear* Dora, what a *blessing* you've come! Now you will be ready to amuse dear Edward for a bit and I shall be able to get on with some work. I simply *must* go into Great Malvern and do some business.'

The study door upstairs opened:

'Is that Dorabella? Why can't you come up instead of gassing down there?'

When I went up he asked:

'How's Wolverhampton? Come and tell me all about it. Going to football matches is far nicer than all this mouldy music.' Then later: 'Let's go out: have you brought your bicycle?' So off we went somewhere.

'I want to be amused, so just make haste and begin.'

It is terribly difficult to have to begin 'amusing' anybody—like turning on a tap—especially when one's best efforts are greeted with a sort of grunt; but I usually managed to think of something that pleased him and we generally came home happier than when we went out.

The Elgars spent Christmas 1901 in Düsseldorf and there was a performance of *Gerontius* under Professor Buths, the first on the Continent. Mr. Jaeger went over to it with them, and he wrote me a long account of it in a letter dated 29 December 1901:

We travelled to D'dorf together & had a lovely passage. Buths and a friend met us & we drove to 17 Ehrens Strasse a nice house & a comfortable one. Buths, his Frau Professor & his 2 daughters were as kind as kind could be. On Wednesday morning we went to the first orchestral rehearsal with Soloists. The orchestra of 80 odd was not like Wood's 110 for reading powers or tone, but they answered every purpose & Elgar had not very much to find fault with. Buths, though a man of complete savoir faire is not a great 'interpreter'—I mean co-creator, and there were many passages of which more might have been made as regards mystery, feeling, expression, force, etc. etc. Still, one can't always have everything, & time is an important factor at a Rehearsal. But directly Wüllner opened his mouth to sing 'Jesus, Maria, meine Stunde kam' we said that man has Brains. And by the Olympian Jove he had Brains galore. He made us sit up and realise that Elgar's intention, & what I had expected when I wrote my much maligned analysis, could be realised by an artist. I never heard such intellectual deeply felt singing. Not that W's voice is wonderful. No! But his Brains & his heart are; & they are more than mere voice in a work of such greatness as this wonderful Gerontius. We were delighted & moved to tears. As for dear Mrs. E., you can imagine her state of seventh-heaven-beatitude, with eyebrow lifting, neck twisting, forget-me-not glances towards the invisible Heavens! Don't think I am making fun of her! I am not; but you know her signs of deep emotion over the Dr's music don't you? There was another Rehearsal with Chorus in the evening. The audience (admitted on payment) was quite considerable & the applause ditto. Buths introduced E. to the Chorus, as he had introduced him to the Orchestra in the mg., and everybody seemed in the best of spirits. Then, next (Thursday) mg., there was another Orchestral Rehearsal when Buths filed & E interfered more frequently to secure readings more in accordance with his conceptions. Then in the evening, the Event. The Hall was crammed full though it was a beastly night (there is no more polite word for it). The Hall is a fine one, and acoustically superb. We (E., Mrs. E, A. Johnstone of the Manchester Guardian, & yours truly) sat in the third row of the balcony right facing the Orchestra and we heard marvellously well. Every little detail came out beautifully & I can assure you I have not had such an elevating soul-stirring experience for years as listening under such circumstances to this wonderful music. The Chorus was perfect, there is no other word for it. The effect of the pp 12 part passages sung dead in tune (throughout the week) was quite ethereal, while the ff tutti were thundered out with imposing force & splendid sonority. They speak of the 'Rhineland tone' among Choruses in Germany & I realised here, where the beauty of the tone lay. It is in a remarkable roundness & sweetness in the female voices & by a big sonority in the male. For though the trousered contingent in the Choir was by <u>no</u> <u>means</u> large, the quantity of tone produced by it was quite sufficient, even for the terrific Dämonen Chorus. That masterful piece, which was so completely ruined at B'ham, was given with perfect ease & yet with strenuous dramatic force which one could not possibly realise through studying the music on paper. Wüllner did not seem in very good voice & he made one serious blunder; but these were only as blots on a summer sun. Elgar was very nearly called after Part I, & during the long pause (20 minutes or more) he held a reception in the 'Soloisten-Zimmer', where I was told many musicians from other towns congregated to congratulate E. & Buths. I alas! was not there, for I was waylaid by my many D'dorf friends who all wanted to shake hands & ask questions & stand me Bottles of Hock which I didn't want. In fact, I didn't want <u>them</u> either, but what was I to do? In any case, I missèd the chance of speaking to the 'auswärtige' musicians, as I ought to have done, & wanted to do. So I didn't bless my D'dorf friends exactly. In Part 2 Wüllner was <u>great</u>, especially in the 'Take me away'. The big Chorus 'Praise to the Holiest' which astonished the German musicians by its monumental architecture, was a masterly performance & the Finale, that wonderful Finale, was another revelation to those who heard it only at B'ham. Unfortunately the Angel was anything but angelically perfect. But though Elgar suffered sundry twitches & pangs when the Angel threatened to 'fall', the audience could not have realised, thanks to Buths' alertness, how dangerously near collapse the performance came once or twice through this d—— Angel's shortcomings. (By the way, what the Musical Times says about her, <u>I</u> did <u>not</u> telegraph). Well, at the end E was enthusiastically called, & though he had to fight his way through thronging crowds of people down the stairs & to the front, the applause & shouts were kept up until <u>at last</u> (the time seemed a small eternity) he reached the Podium. There the Chorus & Orchestra & Organ joined in a <u>Tusch</u> & a large fine laurel wreath was handed to him. He asked Buths (so the latter told me) what to do with the thing! Directly I saw the wreath presented I rushed out, took a cab to the Telegraph office & wired 400 words to the Times. Yes, <u>The</u> Times, the account which you read. How it came about that <u>I</u> wired to the Times is too long a tale to tell here; but in addition to doing E & B & the firm a jolly good turn, I earned <u>20 Marks</u>! Unfortunately, another wire which I sent to the Central

News was much mutilated by that agency & only a few papers thought the event of sufficient importance to give the 8 or nine lines to it. So much for the English appreciation of High art in music. If this had only been Dan Leno's first appearance in Germany there would have been columns in all the English papers. Ye Gods! You have to do a lot yet to be considered a musical nation. Your Editors are at fault. After the Concert there was a Supper, but I got to that rather late, because of my work at the Telegraph office. In my absence Buths had made a speech about E, and my inducing him (B) to take an interest in English music, etc. etc. When I came back at last (about 11.15) I was placed between the Angel & her Sister. (I have never been so near feeling good.) She, the poor Angel, was very depressed, for cruel, wicked Buths had told her during the performance & after she had missed an important entry, that 'es war scheusslich'. Pretty strong that! I said some nice things about her nice voice (it is a nice voice) & the difficult part & then we became good friends at once. (Of course! you will say.) Well, it was a jolly, most enjoyable evening. Elgar confessed to me he had never had such an one! He made a nice, quiet, modest speech of thanks & appreciation to Buths, Wüllner, & me! & I blushed (tried to) as in duty bound; & at 1.30 or so we at last drove home, having spent an exciting, beautiful day. I wish you & Mrs. Baker & a few other English friends had been there to see how my countrymen, my townsmen, honoured our Doctor. It was everywhere 'Hochverehrter Meister' & 'Geehrter Meister'; E's eyes twinkled thereat. On Friday we were all invited to Carl Sohn's, a rich D'dorf painter. We had a gorgeous feast. Talk about Rudesheimer!! We were 3 hours or so over Dinner, a number of painters & musicians having been invited to meet E. On Saturday Buths, E, Johnstone & myself went to Cologne to visit old Dr. Franz Wüllner, the Director of the Cologne Conservatoire & conductor of the Gürzenich Concerts. He all but promised definitely to produce Gerontius at his first Concert next year. In the evening I sped homewards. I could tell you lots of other interesting details of our delightful stay at beautiful D'dorf, but I must stop. I have sent you a Manchester Guardian giving Johnstone's critique (Very Good!) Next month (February) the M. T. will bring much more about the conspicuous event. The firm appreciate all I have done, the Directors made me nice speeches & have doubled my usual Xmas Box. And now Farewell & say a pretty thank you for this ausführlichen account of our journey. You have never had such a long letter I bet. . . .

Yours very sincerely
RODNIM

The Lower Rhine Music Festival took place at Düsseldorf in May 1902, and the Elgars and Mr. Jaeger went there again for it. There was another splendid performance of *Gerontius* and this time the 'Angel' music was sung by Miss Muriel Foster. The exuberant letter in which Mr. Jaeger told me of her success and of the pæan of praise she drew from Professor Buths is, alas, one of those which has been destroyed. They brought back from Düsseldorf two huge laurel wreaths tied with coloured ribbon, with *Niederrheinisches Musik Fest* printed on each ribbon in silver. These were hung up in the study and the Lady showed them to me with much pride. *His* account of it all and how the wreaths were presented lost nothing in the telling. He said he saw them coming—apparently by themselves—as he stood, somewhat embarrassed, on the platform with everyone making a noise. Then he saw that they were being borne by a small man who handed them over to an official. Finally they got to him; and what to do with them he couldn't think—one on each side of him, 'like cartwheels'!

How strange it seems now that the first London performance of *Gerontius* was not till June 1903, when it was done in Westminster Cathedral, the next being at the Elgar Festival at Covent Garden in 1904.

On 10 May 1902 there was a Worcester Philharmonic Concert, and Herr E. Ettling was tympanist. He was a highly competent amateur. He came with us to the Hydes' and did conjuring tricks after tea. E. E. called him 'Uncle Klingsor' because of his magic arts.

On Monday, 12 May, E. E. wrote:

My dear Dorabella

Sorry to see so little of you on Saturday. We did not stir today

because I am ill with a cold. (Felsnaptha is the <u>moneyback</u> soap)
Don't forget this, or me who am

Your inferior friend

ED. ELGAR

Why <u>did</u> you wear the same clothes as last May & May before?

(The answer to that one is, of course, that I didn't!)

So many people have asked me what the allusion to Felsnaptha Soap means that I feel I should explain that it was a
household soap much advertised at that time—good for pots
and pans but not for persons. We saw some in a village shop
window one day and E. E. was greatly tickled by the wording
on the packet. He insisted on my going in and buying some as
he wanted to take it home. It amused me that nothing would
induce him to go into the shop and buy it himself, but he gave
me the money and I made the purchase. However, the smell of
it was too much for us and he tore the wrapper off and put it in
his pocket, throwing the soap over a hedge. When we got
home he went straight to the Lady. I was not present, but I
heard sounds of horror and expostulation followed by a burst
of laughter and I fancied that E. E. must have suggested a new
bath soap! Later, I was not exactly scolded but it was hinted
that we had both been 'rather naughty', and I noticed that E. E.
appeared at tea in another coat.

On 16 June I was summoned to Malvern again by telegram.
I went down next day and found the poor little Lady in bed,
laid up with a horrid feverish cold. Of course she was fidgeting
about E. E., and having someone there to keep him cheerful
made her comparatively happy and care-free. He and I had
some bicycle rides, and sat by the Severn, and I heard a lot of
music in the evenings: the *Coronation Ode* and, of course, *The
Apostles*. He wanted to hear all about the Wolverhampton
Exhibition and said he should come to it, chiefly, I think, to see
the loan collection of pictures at the Art Gallery, and with a
view to some of the side-shows. However, he did not come to

BIRCHWOOD LODGE,
NEAR MALVERN.

TELEGRAMS:
LEIGH SINTON.

CRAEG LEA,
WELLS ROAD,
MALVERN.

TELEGRAMS:
UPPER WYCHE

Oct 15. 02

Dear Miss Penny:

(That's not right-.)

Dear Miss Dorabella,

(That's feeble)

My dear Dorabella

(piff! very ordinary)

now for it —

My dear Adorable
Donabellissima,

(That will do)
oncemore, My

My dear adorable

Dorabellissima!

(Gosh! 2½ a bar)

I quite forget what I was going to say.

Or!

This is it.

I believe that an association freewheel Gallery of for the pictures of Bicycles —

This one wrong!

Bismillah!

I am told that a gallery of loan

- freewheel exhibition football Bicycles

       (Dear me.)

  Look here!

I want to see <u>You</u>!

(No, I don't).

I want to come to
    Wolverhampton. Yah!

1. I want to see the pictures

2. I want to see the Exhibition

3. I want to know about
    freewheels tif my bike
    is worth converting (I
    trow not) is it being it.

4. I want to run in a football
    <u>association</u> match.

noted the same day.

5. I want food & drink
& decent <u>cigarette</u>

6. I want a coherent
reply to this quick

7. I do not want any
reflections on the
legibility of this letter

8. I send my respects
to the house
including (unnecessary)
the recipient.

9. I kiss your hand

Jean (salaaming)

your devoted

it, though the Lady and Carice came on 25 July. The day after I left Malvern he wrote:

22 June 02 . . . I have had my tyres 'going-on-into-their-3rd-season'; 1300 miles. Ought I to buy new ones or will these last without

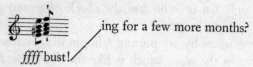

ffff bust!

ing for a few more months?

Yours very truly

ED: ELGAR

P.S. I rode 50 miles (who with?) yesterday without a curse-book out all day. Lovely but lonely. (I was solus.)

His letter dated October 15th is reproduced in facsimile.

It was in quite early days at Craeg Lea that E. E. began to be bothered by receiving manuscripts from budding composers. Later he was really snowed under with them, and he was driven to have a slip printed to the effect that Dr. Elgar regretted that he could not consider any manuscript composition unless accompanied by a personal introduction.

A particularly dreadful one had come by post one morning:

'Do come and listen to this, Dorabella; you never heard anything like it.'

It was a march song and it had a horribly blatant refrain. After playing it with gusto he snatched it up and hit me over the head with it.

'Oh! come along: let's go out.'

I used to be rather sorry for the people who sent the things, and I said so. I expect they had taken great pains and thought they were lovely. Looking through some that had been opened but not dealt with, I found one which rather attracted me.

'This is really not at all bad,' I said. 'He's got quite a nice melody.'

'Bring it here—let me see it.' He glanced through it. 'It's

very ordinary and the nice melody you talk of is straight out of Beethoven.'

'Well, if you put Chopin in *Gerontius*——'

I'd done it now. Afterwards I wondered if I was glad or sorry. I felt that he ought to know what people said, and probably I was the only person who had the cheek or temerity to tell him.

'What do you mean by my putting Chopin in *Gerontius*?'

So I told him of the place which is like the *Polonaise Fantaisie*.

'I know nothing about pianoforte music. I hate the piano as an instrument and I don't care for Chopin and I never heard the piece you mention.'

I determined that I would never speak of anything of the sort again, but on one occasion I gave myself away quite involuntarily. We were going through the proofs of the *Coronation Ode* and he came to 'Daughter of Ancient Kings'. I felt as if turned to stone and I know I went white.

'How do you like that?——What's the matter?'

I said I thought it was charming, but I knew the beginning quite well.

'What *do* you mean?'

'It begins like a hymn in the Ancient and Modern book.'

'What hymn? I don't know anything about your hymns. Can you play it?'

So I stretched across him and played the first line of 528. 'The likeness only goes so far,' I said.

'Well, I can't help it. I've never heard the wretched hymn in my life.'

'I am quite sure you haven't,' I said; 'it's only a coincidence.'

On 21 December 1902, he wrote:

Dear Miss

Being a pennytential week, I drop the Dorabella & varying conjugations of it as being worldly & somewhat profane: not that it is as bad as D——, or, even, ——: but dear Miss, its not proper for

Lent—only this is Advent or something. Yes: Advent. I've just looked it up in the Ency: Brit: (10th Edition 35 volumes) and (and mark you) a revolving book-case.

(A present! dearie—I mean dear Miss). Persons—the elect—admitted to this Study—revolve 3 times before entering—in honour of (me and) the Bookcase.

Oh! Child, I know things now—35 volumes.

Dear Miss: won't you come & see them? 35 Revolving volumes. Oh! Law! My head goes round.

Dear Miss: it is too lovely for words & its my very own.

This is Xmas sirloinidly frivolous—forgive me.

My best wishes for Xmas to you all. I say: dear Miss: I have a Butterfly—alive & flying round the room. He's a beauty & drinks sugar & water at my request & also lives in 35 revolving volumes —I'm off again.

I hope you can read this—I cannot—and you bar the typewriter & it put Dorabellissima so sweetly prettily.

believe me Dear Miss

Yours furtively & revolvingly

ISAAC NEWTON ELGAR (35 volumes)

When I was talking over plans for this book with Carice Elgar-Blake in 1936 and seeing if she approved of the selection of letters that I had chosen for inclusion and reproduction we came to the one about the revolving book-case.

'Do you know,' I said, 'I never saw that book-case? I was not able to leave home that time when they asked me. What became of it?'

'Mother had to send it away quite soon. Father would turn it round so!'

I can well imagine the scene. How I should have loved to have been there and turned it round with him! I expect it would have been another of those occasions when we made such a noise that the Lady would have appeared at the door to find out what we were doing. Sometimes she used to stay and laugh too for a bit and then go away and leave us to it. But when visitors were there she often gave me the impression that she was laughing out of politeness because they were so much amused—and perhaps it would soon stop! I have heard her apologize to people as though they might not quite understand or appreciate his jokes and fun:

'Oh *please* don't mind him. Edward dear, how *can* you?'

It has even been said to me—which was very funny considering how often we met:

'Don't attend to him, Dora dear, he doesn't mean it.' After which remark E. E. and I exploded, and I was terrified lest she should think it rude of me. However, she seemed not to mind a bit, which was a great relief to my mind.

I only stayed one night with the Elgars in 1903 and that not till late in October. I was ill early in the year and spent most of March and April in Marseilles, at the house of a cousin who was British Vice-Consul. On 27 February I had a letter from E. E. which ends:

. . . & now in haste, a safe journey, a pleasant visit & a safer & pleasanter return to your sorrowing (!?!?) friends one of whom (?which) is Edward Elgar.

On 21 March I had a letter from the Lady—a typed one and a great improvement on a previous effort.

Craeg Lea   Malvern   18 March 1903

My dear Dora

We were very glad to hear from you and that you are there safe and well, it must be very interesting and delightful to see all the shipping. The photo you sent is beautiful, but rather expensive! costing 3 pence extra postage! I have been wishing to write but have been so busy; I really have a great deal to do just now, H. E. is so busy with his work. I do what writing I can for him. Such wonderful things have been written since you were here, and there is a good deal in print now.

H. E. has only been away for Hanley, we had a horrid journey there it took really <u>hours</u>, but the Hotel was very nice and the nice warm hearted Hanley people were enormously excited and could not make enough of 'the Dr.' E. had a splendid Chorus rehearsal the first evening, the Chorus is magnificent, so fresh and spontaneous and seemed to know all the music by heart. E. had no trouble and they took all his 'nuances' at once. Next day Mr. Martin and Mr. Littleton joined us, so all was congenial. At the P. M. rehearsal Mr. Ettling appeared with the Hallé orch. absolutely beaming after their wonderful evening at Manchester.

You know Gerontius was postponed for a week as Coates was ill, we were to have gone, but of course had to be at Hanley on the postponed day. It is of no use to try to tell you all they tell us, you must see the papers, the impression must have been tremendous and they at once decided to repeat it early next autumn. To return to Hanley. First came Froissart beautifully played, then Sea Pictures, (3) and two choruses, and then a reception in the Mayor's Parlour, then back to the Hall and then a most beautiful performance of Gerontius. I think I never heard anything more lovely than the beginning of the Kyrie and so it went on, simply splendid and such enthusiasm.

We returned next day and had hours more travelling.

H. E.'s new bike came after a month's waiting for it, it looked superb and he tried it and liked it much, went off for a real ride and it all went wrong and has to be sent back. It is so stupid.

He has wretched lumbago today I am sorry to say, I hope it will soon go. We had a good Phil. practice yesterday in spite of torrents of rain, you must come to the concert all being well, and hear the Bavarians, they are sung with such joy. I am afraid I have made many mistakes but I am writing in a hurry and rather tired. I hope you do not dislike a typed letter, but I thought it less tiring to do.

Now, dear Dora, come home safe and well and please look much better.

With love and mind you take care of yourself and not be too 'venturesome', let us hear of you.

Your affecte:

C. ALICE ELGAR (MRS.)!

At the bottom, in E. E.'s writing:

3d to pay! Are you worth it? Much love to the Mistral.

E. E.

3 September found me in London for the day between visits to Buckinghamshire and Sussex. I lunched with Mr. Jaeger and went with him to the Hereford Festival rehearsal at the then

new St. James's Hall. The gallery was full of interesting people —composers waiting to rehearse their own work, soloists, conductors, and musicians of all sorts. As we came through the doorway he remarked:

'Someone should announce us: "Nimrod and Dorabella!" All faces would be turned this way!'

Mr. Jaeger was of course greeted by all we came near. I knew several people, but many others by sight only. I saw the Lady sitting in the front row. I did not see E. E., but evidently he saw us come in, for I found him behind me when I got to a seat.

'Hullo! What are *you* doing here?'

They were rehearsing the Tchaikovsky Fifth Symphony and there was a pause between two movements. E. E. slipped into an empty seat next to me.

He seemed to like the Waltz movement, particularly towards the end.

'Do you know this? You'll like it,' taking a fresh grip of my arm (which was extraordinarily painful) and holding up a warning finger. When the Symphony was over E. E.'s turn came, and we saw him arrive at the conductor's desk to rehearse the *Variations*. The Lady came and sat by me, full of anxiety and despair at the lateness of the hour, and an almost tragic fear that there would not be time enough for a satisfactory rehearsal. However, all seemed to be well, and it was most interesting and delightful being there.

On 14 October 1903, *The Apostles* was produced at the Birmingham Festival. Everyone was looking forward to this when it became known that Elgar was going to conduct it himself. Critics and friends alike said:

'Let us see what the composer can do with his own music.'

We were not disappointed. What a difference from *Gerontius* in 1900! The Chorus had learnt their lesson and they did themselves—and the work—justice. The Town Hall was packed. I did not see the Elgars that day to speak to, but had tea with them at the Grand Hotel on the Friday, after the B minor Mass.

On 30 October I went down to Malvern and we had a glorious evening of music.

Next day we went to a concert at the Imperial Hotel and heard the Brodsky String Quartet. I sat with E. E. and the Ninepin. At tea afterwards I was introduced to Adolf Brodsky. E. E. took him by the arm and said:

'Mr. Brodsky, I want to introduce you to Dorabella of my *Variations.*'

Adolf Brodsky swung round and nearly dropped his tea-cup. I entirely forget what he said, or what language he said it in, but he beamed with delight and gesticulated with the tea-cup in one hand and a sandwich in the other. I really thought he would drop both.

The Elgars went to Alassio early in December and spent Christmas there.

In 1904 many important things happened. The Elgar Festival at Covent Garden took place in March. Unfortunately I could not go to this or to the rehearsal for which E. E. had sent me a card. My absence at this Festival has been remarked on by several people. The Elgars seemed quite hurt about it and Mr. Jaeger thought it extraordinary. It was no use giving them the real reason why I could not go as they would not have understood, so I just said I was very sorry that I could not be there on account of 'other engagements'—and left it at that.

My family had strict rules in regard to the proper observance of Lent. All invitations to balls, parties, and entertainments were declined as being out of keeping with the season. I was quite used to this as I had been brought up to consider it the right thing. We went to lectures but not to concerts. The only music we heard or took part in during Lent was sacred music, and usually performed in church. But performances of *The Messiah* or Bach's *Passion* Music were considered exceptions. Now picture the day when our Wolverhampton Choral Society decided to perform *Gerontius* on a date in Lent. When I heard it had been settled my heart sank, and I did my utmost to get the date altered, but it was not possible. When the invitation of the Committee came to me to be one of the sopranos in the Semi-Chorus the matter had to be settled at once, so I approached my father on the subject and the following conversation ensued:

'You know quite well that we don't go to musical entertainments in Lent.'

'But this is sacred music.'

'Is it?'

'The words are sacred.'

'Some of them may be. But it is called a "Dream"; I should call it a nightmare; and it isn't true—which is one mercy. Do you call *that* sacred?'

(My father had been to the production of *Gerontius* at Birmingham and was greatly bored. It was many years later that he was persuaded to hear it a second time and I am glad to say that the excellence of that performance did a good deal to improve opinions.)

'If it was the *Messiah*', I said, rather foolishly, 'you wouldn't mind my singing in it even though it was not in church?'

'Now you are not going to pretend that the *Dream of Gerontius* by your friend Dr. Elgar is on a par with the *Messiah*?'

This was rather a facer. What I wanted to say would have been so unacceptable that it would only have made matters worse, so the volume of words that longed for utterance was stifled, and I beat a hasty retreat in silence and resigned myself to the inevitable.

I don't suppose my people had any idea what I went through after that; my own intense disappointment; what was said in the town and the wonder expressed on all sides, as I naturally preferred to justify my father's ruling on the matter. Then, of course, I had to write and explain it all to the Elgars. I was allowed to sing at the rehearsals, but perhaps I need hardly add that it was not in the *Semi*-Chorus that I sang.

I do not wish it to be thought for one moment that I recall this story as a complaint against my father. The interest of it lies, in my opinion, in the light that it casts on the position of a composer *vis-à-vis* his more elderly contemporaries.

Anybody who has attended the Three Choirs' Festivals during the last thirty years cannot fail to have noticed the extraordinary influx of the elderly and inflexible when either *Elijah* or *Messiah* are to be performed.

The Lady wrote me a wonderful description of the Festival —the Chorus all in white with their pink and blue sashes, and the masses and masses of flowers. The music was wonderful and she was delighted with the whole thing. I had a letter from Nimrod:

37 Curzon Road, W. 27/iii/4

My dear Dora

... Why the Beelzebub didn't you come to that unique Festival? ... They played you beautifully & the audience liked you hugely. They liked me too, though they only murmured approval, that peculiar audible sigh of approval which oftens means more than applause. They applauded You, though. The new overture is beautiful & new, & shows a surer touch than almost anything else I know of E. E.'s. The Apostles impressed me tremendously though nothing 'came off' as the composer meant it. The acoustic defects of the theatre were too great. I sat near dear Mrs. Baker, & we twain cried silently & shyly over the marvellous beauties of the various scenes. You don't consider me a softy or an old woman, because I can still be moved to tears by the happiness of letting such beauty 'creep in my ears' do you? I say, that analysis of mine isn't a bad guess at things. I have without a performance anticipated the effect & beauties very correctly, though I say so ('cos no one else does). Even the 'Guardian' critic, Talbot, after pitching frightfully into me in October confesses that things sound quite different now (after he has studied the work, doubtless with my analysis—read his remarks!) I smile. Elgar had a <u>rare</u> time and everything was splendid. Ask dear little Mrs. E. She must have been in the 7th Heaven of Happiness. <u>Such</u> swells they met, from the Queen downwards. A great time for E. E. & some of us who have believed in him & fought for him (I had to fight hard for him at Novello's) are happy. I have been asked to write a book (chiefly critical) on Elgar. Will you help me? I hope to see something of you when you come to town. Meanwhile kindest regards to you and Miss Danks.[1]

Ever yours
NIMROD

The Apostles was done in Birmingham on 14 April and it was a fine performance. We went over from Wolverhampton and saw the Elgars afterwards. They told us that they were going to Cologne in May for a performance there, and subsequently I had a card from E. E. with a picture of the Gürzenich Concert Hall and a message written all round it:

I know you don't want this, but I send it with much love. The Apostles comes off here tomorrow. Mosshead is here & Alice & I am very hot & want Bier. Yours Edwd. E.

Two days later I had a card from Nimrod:

Dear Dorabella

We had a magnificent performance of the Apostles. The orchestra (150) especially was gorgeous & for the first time within my experience realised <u>all</u> my anticipations (as expressed in my analysis). E. E. was called out after part 1 (a <u>rare</u> honour here) & <u>twice</u> amid great enthusiasm at end. The chorus was excellent & soloists at least quite adequate. Mrs. E. & E. are delighted.

Yours
NIMROD

I went to Malvern on 15 June and reached Craeg Lea in time for luncheon. E. E. and I spent the afternoon on the British Camp and it was perfectly lovely up there. While we were sit-

---

[1] Of Wolverhampton. Then living in Gloucester: a contralto in the Festival Chorus.

ting quiet, watching for things, a small bird perched on a stony bank close by.

'What's that?' he whispered.

'Whinchat,' I said, greatly daring.

Evidently offended, the bird flew away.

'Whinchat!' E. E. remarked scornfully. 'What do you know about whinchats?'

We had quite an argument about that, but I suspected that I was wrong, and of course I was. It was a stonechat; rather a dirty one and not so well marked as they usually are and I don't think it was really a very bad mistake! However, it was a long time before I heard the last of it. When we got home we settled down to an hour's music, and I think it must have been then that I heard *In the South* all through. I had of course missed it by not being at the Elgar Festival. I found a proof copy—in the rubbish basket—and took it home with me to add to my treasures.

The Ninepin dined and spent the evening, and I heard more about the impending move to Hereford, which was most exciting.

'I've got to go to Hereford to-morrow morning', remarked E. E., 'to do some business: why not come? We might go and see Plâs Gwyn if there's time.'

'Oh, I *should* like to, that would be lovely!' And then, thinking, as I always do, of the places one would see on a new journey, I added:

'What fun! I shall go through the Colwall Tunnel for the first time.'

E. E. nearly choked.

'There's a Cathedral at Hereford and all you think of is a railway tunnel.'

'I know there's a Cathedral and I'm longing to see it, but I've seen trains go into that tunnel from near here so often and seen them go out at the other end when I stayed at the "Westminster Arms", and now at last I'm going to do it myself!' Even the Lady had to laugh at that and Troyte grinned.

Next morning, when we were through the tunnel E. E. exclaimed:

'Well, what on earth you wanted to go through that smoky hole for beats me.'

It was most interesting seeing the Hills from the West side for the first time; it seemed to be lovelier as we went farther away, with the British Camp showing up so splendidly. Fortunately we had the compartment to ourselves and spent most of the time looking out of first one window and then the other. Whether all the things he told me about what we saw on the way to Hereford were really true or not—I had my suspicions about some of it—I never found out. It was great fun and the journey came to an end all too soon. I cannot remember if we went to the Cathedral that day after all, but I saw the new house and thought it most attractive, with its veranda covered with climbing roses and honeysuckle, and its charming garden. We went on to the lawn and E. E. seized me suddenly by the arm and said in a sort of stage whisper:

'Bung yirds![1] Look!' A family of young thrushes was being fed on the lawn under the cedar-tree.

On 24 June 1904, my diary has just one line: 'Sir Edward Elgar.'

[1] Often, in early summer, when we were out together, he would say, 'Come on, let's look for "bung yirds"!' The sound of the words pleased him.

SIR EDWARD ELGAR

June 1904

PLÂS GWYN

THE Elgars left Malvern in the summer of 1904 and, after a short holiday abroad, settled down at Plâs Gwyn, Hereford. The postcard which I had from Corfu said, 'Come to Hereford and see us soon', and at the end of August I went there for three days. I found the Lady and Carice in possession—Sir Edward was in London—and I went all over the house and was shown everything and found old friends in new places.

'The Indian furniture has positively come into its own here,' I said. 'Doesn't it look nice?'

The study was a fine large room on the ground floor. It had a bow window looking out on the veranda and another window which let in the morning sunshine. When I first went into it I could not help thinking of the tiny study at Forli, and I spoke my thoughts aloud, adding, as we stood there arm in arm: 'Isn't it glorious to feel how he has got on, and how people all over the world are beginning to understand and appreciate?'

I looked round the room with interest; found the 'green books' and other treasures, and I noticed much that was new.

'I think *great* music can be written here, dear Dora, don't you?'

Then we had tea and a tremendous talk about Italy, music, and the Archives; and later on, when we had watered the garden, we settled down to a quiet evening.

That night I had much to think of. I liked finding them in this nice house. It was larger and far more comfortable than Craeg Lea, and I was glad to realize that things seemed to be improving for them all round. Royalties were coming in more freely and, consequently, ends met more easily. It was so good for them both to be able to go abroad more frequently, and they were making more and more friends every year. In the old days the little Lady so often looked worried and tired, though she never complained; in fact it was always difficult to find out if she was worried about anything special. If any one was tiresome she never spoke of it, and bothers and worries were never mentioned. Once when I was at Malvern I asked how a certain rather tiresome business had been settled, and the Lady drew herself up and said: 'We won't talk about that, I think, dear Dora,' and as she spoke her face became set in an odd sort of way, her large blue eyes staring straight in front of her into vacancy. That was what E. E. used to call her 'stony image' look.

Talking to their daughter recently I was asking about things, and she remarked how difficult it was to find out about business affairs during Malvern and Hereford days, as no mention was ever made in a diary of anything disagreeable or vexing.

After breakfast next morning I heard the Lady in the study opening and shutting windows, and then she came out and shut the door behind her.

'Do go into the study, dear Dora, there's such a surprise in there.'

I wondered if she had been moving furniture and, if so, why she had not asked me to help her; however, I opened the door and went in. I was greeted with a burst of music! But what curious music it was, and very difficult to describe. It was rather like a harp, and the sound rose and fell in arpeggios of intervals of thirds—minor or diminished. It was very strange and rather eerie—in an empty room. I walked forward and saw that one of the windows which looked on the veranda was only partly open and a framework with vertical strings was fixed in the opening. I wondered if it was an Æolian Harp—I had never seen or heard one. The Lady had come in after me and was now beside me.

'Edward loves it. He thinks it is so soothing!'

'I don't think it would "soothe" me,' I said; 'it varies too much; but I call it most fascinating.'

A little breeze sprang up and it seemed as though a second harp joined in with the first.

PLÂS GWYN, HEREFORD

CARICE ELGAR ON THE VERANDA

September 1st, 1904

'That's jolly. What does it do when there is a high wind? I should think it would get tremendously excited.'

'We don't generally have that window open when it blows, and if it gets excited Edward takes it down. The cadences are lovely, aren't they, dear Dora? So ethereal and mystic!'

I had my bicycle with me and I went down into Hereford twice that day doing errands for the Lady—chose some material for curtains, and made them, and also helped with some dressmaking; and the following evening His Excellency came home. My diary says: 'He was very tired but thoroughly cheerful. He brought back a huge box of sweets for her Ladyship from Professor Sanford.'[1]

It was still hot and lovely next day and E. E. and I rode about the lanes on our bicycles. He took me to Holm Lacy, and we sat by the river Wye and talked about all sorts of things. It was here that I first learnt the story of the 'Nimrod' Variation.

'There's going to be some fun in Hereford to-morrow. It's the finals of the Small Car Trials. Shall we go? Fishface will like it, we'll take her too.'

It was rather fun, but in 1904 cars were getting so much more reliable that the breakdowns one heartlessly hoped for seldom happened. I went home that evening—bag, baggage, and bicycle.

On 6 January 1905, I had a sad little letter from Nimrod: he was ordered to Davos immediately for a three months' cure. I spoke of it in my next letter to His Excellency but got no answer, though I am sure he thought very gravely of the news. Then, in May, I had a card from Nimrod saying that he was leaving Davos and meeting Mrs. Jaeger at Luzern, adding, 'I am not quite Healed, alas!'

I had had a good many letters and cards from E. E. during that winter on the subject of music for my string orchestra. Some were helpful, some were not, as witness this postcard of 3 March:

[1] Professor S. S. Sanford, Yale University, U.S.A.

No, you mayn't, Yes. Yes, you may, No. I think it would be —— No, you may. Yes, you may not. Upon thinking it over I conclude that —— After further consideration I feel that it would be better to —— You might know that my advice is final; please do just as I say. E. E.

I also had a letter dated 8 October 1904, recommending me to do Handel's 'Water Music'. It ends:

I like the old Water Music, but I take a little old rye with it now. Yours dispertinently, E. E.

I went to Hereford for a short visit in April 1905. E. E. was in London and was expected home that evening. The Lady and I were in the study together after tea and I remember seeing a copy of the *Introduction and Allegro for Strings* on the table. Turning the pages over eagerly, I wanted to know all about it.

'I missed hearing this the other day, what is it like?' I asked.

'Oh! it's *very* wonderful, dear Dora! He wrote most of it when we were in Wales.'

'When is it going to be done again?' (pause). I seemed to feel that she was not happy about something, and I looked up at her as I finished my question. She had that set expression of hers—her 'stony image' look—'Nothing has been settled yet. I think you had better not ask!'

I thought this very odd. I had seen no press-notices as they had not yet been sent to me. When E. E. came home that evening there was so much to hear and to talk about that there was no opportunity to speak of the new work, but next day, when I was in the study alone, I found the score in the same place on the table and began looking at it again. I was so completely engrossed in it that I had not heard His Excellency come into the room.

'It's no use your looking at that.'

(I knew quite well what he meant; that I could never attempt it with my string orchestra.)

'I know we could not play it *now*, but one day perhaps?...'

'No day.'

'Couldn't we do it if we asked Max Mossel to bring his Quartet and play it with us? Wouldn't that be all right?'

'Max Mossel would be all right.'

'You *are* horrid! Surely one ought to aim high? [pause]. Oh! *of course* I know we never possibly could! I was only joking.'

I shut up the score and went across to him; I saw that he was worried.

'Do please tell me about it,' I begged.

'That's good stuff. Nothing better for strings has ever been done—and they don't like it.'

Who 'they' were I never knew; I did not ask. I did what comforting I could. As a matter of fact much of what I said then was absolutely prophetic—writing as I am of it now, forty years afterwards. I saw that he did not want to talk about it so I never referred to it again.

I read all the press-notices eagerly when they came to me; something was wrong somewhere, and I never got to the bottom of it. Only in later years did I begin to understand, when I heard the *Introduction and Allegro* superbly played, I realized that the composer had probably never heard it played like that— as he meant it to be. For one thing it was practically impossible in those days to get sufficient rehearsals for any single performance, and besides, to try to perform a work of this difficulty with anything but a first-rate string quartet and orchestra is a forlorn hope.

The fact that the *Introduction and Allegro* was not really a success at the first performance (Queen's Hall, 8 March 1905) may be the reason why the programme note on that occasion, supplied by the composer himself, seems to have been forgotten. There have been letters to the papers from various people making suggestions as to where the themes of the music were first heard and the circumstances under which they were heard, whereas the truth of the matter stares me in the face as I look at the programme! It is an Elgar programme, conducted by the composer. I give the whole of it as it is interesting for many reasons:

Part I   'In the South (Alassio)'
Funeral March (Diarmid & Grania)
Song Cycle 'Sea Pictures' (sung by Miss Ada Crossley)
March in C minor 'Pomp and Circumstance' op. 39, no. 3.
(First time of performance)

Part II Cockaigne
Introduction and Allegro for String Orchestra op. 47.
(First time of performance)
Variations 'Enigma' (op. 36)

Organist Mr. J. E. Borland, F.R.C.O.

The 'Historical and Analytical Notes' were compiled by Edgar F. Jacques and F. Gilbert Webb.

The following is a copy of the 'Note' in the programme.

Introduction and Allegro in G minor and major (op. 47) for Strings
(Orchestra and Quartet)
('A smiling with a sigh!')[1]
(Dedicated to his friend Professor S. S. Sanford,
Yale University, U.S.A.)
(First time of performance)

Writing from Hereford concerning this work in January last, the composer says:

'Some three years ago, in Cardiganshire, I thought of writing a brilliant piece for string orchestra. On the cliff, between blue sea and blue sky, thinking out my theme, there came up to me the sound of singing. The songs were too far away to reach me distinctly, but one point common to all was impressed upon me, and led me to think, perhaps wrongly, that it was a real Welsh idiom—I mean the fall of a third—

'Fitting the need of the moment I made the tune which appears in the Introduction and in the coda of this work; and so my gaudery

[1] *Cymbeline*, Act IV, scene ii.

became touched with romance. The tune may therefore be called, as is the melody in the overture *In the South*, a *canto popolare*, but the suggesting country in this case is Wales, and not Italy.

'The sketch was forgotten until a short time ago, when it was brought to my mind by hearing, far down our own Valley of the Wye, a song similar to those so pleasantly heard on Ynys Lochtyn.[1] The singer of the Wye unknowingly reminded me of my sketch. This I have now completed and, although there may be (and I hope there is) a Welsh feeling in the one theme—to quote Shakespeare again:—"All the waters in Wye cannot wash the Welsh blood out of its body"[2]—the work is really a tribute to that sweet borderland where I have made my home.'

The Elgars went to the States for the first time in July that year (1905), and E. E. sent me a card from Cincinnati. On their return the Lady wrote:

We had a most interesting time, the voyage was lovely, I feel quite ready to start again! I have some Yale notices for you. You must see H. E.'s gorgeous robes! Dear love to all. C. A. E.

At the end of November I went down to Hereford for a few days and when I arrived the Lady met me in the hall. I thought she looked very grave and I wondered what bad news she was going to tell me.

'Dear Dora, it *is* nice to see you, but H. E. is *very* busy and I am afraid you'll have a very dull visit!'

I felt for a moment that she would have been thankful if I had said I would go straight back home there and then; but I didn't say it. Instead I said:

'That's all right! I expect there are heaps of things I can do for you, and if he is busy I can keep you company.'

She seemed a little happier at that and took me upstairs. 'He's hard at work on *The Kingdom*—he's been in the study all this morning and he only had a mouthful of luncheon! I've heard

---

[1] The headland near Llangranog, Cardigan Bay, where the composer was staying.
[2] See *King Henry V*, Act IV, scene vii.

wonderful strains every now and then and it's all such beautiful and exalted music!'

I was pretty sure that she was trying to impress me with the wonder and importance of it all; she feared that my visit might be a distraction to him, and this was a hint to me to keep in the background as much as possible.

I said something appropriate showing that I understood, and she cheered up a bit more.

'Well, make haste and come down, dear Dora. Tea will be ready soon. You remember that when H. E. is busy like this I *never* have a bell rung for meals and we are all as quiet as possible!' (More hints!) I had been with them, of course, at other times when he had had what I irreverently called 'a composing fit', but this one promised to be the best—or worst—that I had experienced so far. The Lady and I had a cosy tea by the fire and had much to say. During tea she filled a thermos flask with tea and put it on a tray that was all set ready, and I noticed that there were eatables in covered muffin-dishes. I sprang up to open the door—I knew it would be useless to offer to take the tray—and she put it down on an oak chest outside the study door. She came back and we finished our tea. 'If H. E. opens the study door he'll see the tray and take it in.'

But no door was opened and no tea was taken in. There was just silence.

I had brought some needlework and I fetched it, and we talked about what I could do for her next day; and so the time slipped away and we went up to dress for dinner.

Dinner was just coming in and the Lady was in the hall when the study door opened and E. E. appeared.

'Where's dinner?' he said rather roughly.

'It's here now, dear darling—we are just going in.'

He looked up and saw me on the stairs:

'Hullo, you here? I'm busy.'

'Yes,' I said, 'so I hear. I'm keeping the Lady company.'

We went in and had our dinner. He never spoke. When he was not looking at his plate he looked straight in front of him with rather a tense expression. He was very pale and looked tired and drawn. Half-way through dessert he pushed his chair back, hit my hand, which happened to be on the table, quite sharply, and left the room. He banged the study door and turned the key. For an instant I thought, 'That's to keep me out!' I looked at the Lady inquiringly.

'He always locks himself in now that the study is downstairs,' she said, 'he feels safer!'

As a matter of fact I never, in all the many times I stayed with them, went into the study unless I was asked, or sent, or unless the door was open.

'Oh, *dear* Dora, look at your *poor* hand! That *was* naughty of Edward, really!'

'It looks much worse than it is,' I said, rubbing it, 'I expect it will be all right soon.'

So we went back to our drawing-room fire, and then began one of the most remarkable evenings I have ever spent.

'Don't you think,' I said, 'that he looked, during dinner, as though he were listening to something far away?'

'What a nice idea, dear Dora! Yes, I do think so.'

Coffee came in and the thermos on the tray was emptied and washed and filled with coffee. I had mine good and strong: I wanted to keep awake. We sat on, talking, reading, working, and when 10.30 came the Lady said:

'Oughtn't you to go to bed, dear Dora? I'm sure you're tired.' But I said please mightn't I stay up with her, I should so much like to. So she said no more about that, for which I was thankful. Presently she said:

'Don't you think it would be nice to make ourselves some tea?' I went with her to the kitchen, and there was a tea-tray all put ready and a large plate of sandwiches covered over, and plates of cake and biscuits. 'It isn't the first time this has happened,' I thought, and carried the tray of eatables into the drawing-room. We had two sandwiches each and took all the rest to the tray on the oak chest.

While we were drinking our tea we heard the piano at last!

The piano in the study was an upright and it stood against the wall with its back to the drawing-room fire-place, and the sound seemed to come down the chimney. As the house was all quiet we heard quite well and we just sat and listened, and forgot the time. It was really most wonderful hearing the scene as it grew, phrase by phrase: once a reminder of something in *The Apostles* —the Lady and I looked at one another—and then it was all new again.

I don't know how long he went on playing, but silence came at length and we both realized that it must be very late and that we were greatly in need of another brew of tea. I went out and made it this time, and the hall clock struck half-past one as I passed it. He was playing again when I came back with the tray, but we had not finished a first cup when the music stopped. We heard his key turn, and the Lady got up and opened the drawing-room door.

'Hullo! You still up? and Dorabella too? and tea! Oh, my giddy aunt! This is good!'

I went and fetched in the other tray and we had a grand meal. He was himself again—quite different from what he had been at dinner. He looked tired, as though he had been through some ordeal, but the ordeal was now over and one could feel what a relief it was.

After we had drunk up all the tea and eaten all the sandwiches and most of the cake and biscuits we went into the study. 'Come and turn over, Dorabella, will you?' and he showed me where part of it was on the back of another page and that sort of thing. Then he played the whole of that evening's work, and more, straight through, and we recognized passages we had heard down the chimney. I saw the words, 'The sun goeth down; Thou makest darkness, and it is night. . . .' When I hear *The Kingdom* now how can I help remembering that evening?

It was well after 2.30 a.m. when I made a move to go to bed.

'I think we'll all go now, dear Dora'—the Lady got up—'I must just go and put things straight in the drawing-room.'

Seeing me make for the door, E. E. called out:

'Oh, do stop and talk to me, Dorabella, I haven't heard half the news yet.'

'Yes, *do* stay, dear Dora, and talk to him; I *promise* not to carry any heavy trays!'

He opened the door for her and I remember the sound of her quick little steps going across the hall.

'Fancy your staying up all that time—why ever did you?'

'I just loved it.'

'You do look charming in that frock. When I saw you on the stairs——'

'I wished I'd brought something quieter and more ordinary, but you see I never bring——'

'Don't you dare to bring any dingy, smoky frocks when you come to stay with me, because I won't stand it——and you only looked at me twice during dinner!'

'Twice, was it? Well, I was terrified! I simply daren't look at you for fear of putting you off your stroke or something.'

'At first I hoped you wouldn't and then, as dinner went on, I hoped you would. Finally I went away; you'd won, and that was why I hit your hand so hard. Did it hurt? I meant it to!'

He picked up my hand and inspected it.

'It stung a bit at first, but there isn't much of a mark left. Here's the Lady. Do you know that it's nearly three to-morrow morning?'

The following day I heard more of *The Kingdom* music. E. E. worked alone all the afternoon, and after tea I helped him with sorting papers in the study.

We heard the postman come and I went to see if there were letters for either of us. The Lady was in the hall.

'One for you, dear Dora, and some dull things for H. E. Will you take them in?'

'What's all that rubbish? I can't be bothered with it.'

'Shall I see what they are?'

73

Most of it was easily disposed of, but I stared at the last one in silence.

'What have you got there?'

'It's from a Temperance Society,' I said. 'They want you to join, and the Secretary encloses a card for the coming season.' Hardly able to speak for sheer joy I put the card down in front of him, adding, 'They've chosen a good motto for their Society, haven't they?' Printed in old English lettering at the top of the card was, 'Hold Thou me up and I shall be safe.'

'That's from the Psalms, isn't it?'

'Yes,' I said, 'the hundred and nineteenth.'

'Could you believe it?' he began—and then I'm afraid we simply exploded with laughter!

I have never known him more delighted with anything. Hearing the noise the Lady came in to know what was the matter. Holding out one hand to her and flourishing the card in the other he called out:

'Come here, Chicky dear, and see what they've sent me!'

The Elgars spent Christmas, 1905, in England, and I had a Christmas card from him from Hereford.

I had sent him a programme of one of my concerts and had a reply dated 18 February 1906.

My dear Child

Many thanks for sending unworthy me your beautiful programme: I have only found, with Troyte's help, fourteen mistakes. I hope all went well and you are happy over it. I should have enjoyed myself—I am not saying anything about the concert—if I could have incogged* (!) myself into the Baths Assembly Rooms for the occasion. My best benison on you and your Orchestra.

Yours very sincerely

EDWARD ELGAR

* new & useful verb!

Curiously enough I forgot to take E. E. to task about the 'fourteen mistakes'. I expect it was because I knew that it was only one of his leg-pulls!

The programmes were works of art and had no mistakes whatever.

The cold of the winter in the Black Country was always rather a trial to me, and I went up to Cumberland on 12 March for a fortnight's change. The entries in my diary during that visit have the word 'Archives' against most days. I remember that I had got rather behind with the work and I took the whole thing—book, parcels, envelopes, and all my paraphernalia—with me. My kind hostess put a table at my disposal which was carried from room to room wherever I wanted it with everything on it undisturbed, and it was covered over with a cloth at night. That was luxury and I got on famously.

Now that the Elgars had left Malvern I did not stay with them nearly so often. Hereford was much farther away and, though not beyond reach by bicycle, the return journey next day, which I had sometimes done from Malvern, would now have been rather an undertaking. I think also that E. E. must have severed his connexion with the Worcester Philharmonic, as I have no record of going to one of those concerts after 1903, and there were no longer, therefore, the opportunities of meeting the Elgars on those delightful days and going back with them afterwards.

The Birmingham Festival of 1906 began on Tuesday, 6 October. There was a glorious performance of *The Apostles* on the Tuesday evening and I saw no empty seat in the Town Hall. The soloists were fine—Agnes Nicholls, Muriel Foster, John Coates, William Higley, Ffrangçon-Davies, and Andrew Black! On Wednesday morning we had *The Kingdom*. My diary refuses to make any comment beyond 'Splendid performance'.

I am afraid I always felt terribly on edge at these first performances of His Excellency's works. I really knew so much of them beforehand and was so anxious that the performance should be as he wished that to sit surrounded by people who criticized without knowledge and made comparisons which only ignorance of the music could account for was exceedingly trying!

Next day the Lady spent the afternoon with us at Wolverhampton and we heard all the news. They had been delighted with the performance of *The Apostles* and *The Kingdom*. We talked about the 'Chair of Music' at Birmingham University and the lectures that His Excellency was giving there and heard many tales of the visit to the States.

In the spring of 1907 I spent six enchanting weeks at the Italian Lakes and was at Cadenabbia for Easter. On my return home I found a card from Cincinnati awaiting me. The Elgars had gone to the States early in April and were there for some time. I did not see them again that summer and had no letters from His Excellency, but I probably heard from the Lady, and again I deplore that so many of her letters have not been preserved.

I was having very sad letters from poor Nimrod. Every winter he was forced to leave England, his family, and his work, and go abroad for treatment. He used to get terribly depressed and downhearted and one began to dread that his health would never be any better. If only he could have stayed on at Davos in 1905 and given the cure a real chance, instead of coming home in May, all might have been well. I had a card from him dated 18 April 1907, from Dr. Brackmann's Sanatorium, Lippspringe, Westfalen:

Many thanks for your kind letter which has been forwarded to me at the above address, where I hope to stay for two months or so. I'm delighted to hear you feel well after your splendid Holiday. Strange! I very nearly went to the Italian Lakes. What a joke if we had met and Oh, what a surprise! I'm here to drink the waters which are supposed to do the lungs good. Nous verrons! I came via Munich, where I spent 3 days (& heard the Joachim quartet—poor Joachim. He really can't any longer.) I liked München muchly & had a nice time, though quiet (very) naturally. When I'm allowed to by my Dr., I'll write you a letter. Meanwhile be a good child & send me the promised continuation of your delightful screed. Ever yours,

NIMROD.

If I could do nothing else for him I could at least write and tell him everything I could think of which might amuse him, and finding that it did so was reward in plenty.

In September, 1907, I went to the Gloucester Festival and stayed with Mr. and Mrs. Danks for it. *The Apostles* on Tuesday evening and *The Kingdom* on Wednesday morning were both very well done. I met the large house-party from Hasfield Court which included my stepmother and Mrs. R. B. Townshend. I had an invitation for myself and two friends to a luncheon given at Beaufort House by the Gloucester Wagon Co. Amy Danks was one of my guests and the other was an aunt, Miss Helen Heale, who had come up from Ross specially to hear *The Kingdom*. In the luncheon interval we saw His Excellency and the Lady and I introduced my guests. I also met Mr. Leo Schuster that day. Speaking of the Shire Hall Concert that evening my diary says: 'Rather dull programme except for Plunket Greene singing Stanford's *Songs of the Sea*. Sat next Mrs. Ludovic Goetz.' (Muriel Foster.)

On Thursday my diary says: 'Luncheon again at Beaufort House & saw Hasfield party. Amy & I went to tea at the Brewers'. The Elgars were there and hosts of people. It was great fun. Mr. Atkins teased A & me about the programme for Worcester pretending that he had all sorts of novelties in prospect—which he hadn't—and "great treats on both the Opening and Closing Days."

"Not really?"

"Yes"—and he edged towards the door to effect a hurried escape— "Elijah and Messiah!" Went to the Lobgesang in the evening & said Goodbye to the Elgars afterwards.'

After the Festival I went down to Devonport for a week to stay with Naval friends and then on to Hereford on 20 September, to find the Lady and E. E.'s niece, Miss Grafton, alone at Plâs Gwyn. His Excellency had been kept in London. I went home next day and had a letter from him:

Edward Elgar

The Athenæum   Pall Mall, S.W.
21 Sept. 1907

My dear Dorabella

I am so sorry that the exigencies of my professional duties——
gosh!

Look here: I couldn't very well manage to come away from town
& missed you: this is sorrow, but of a chastened description as I
shall see you soon, of course: that's all.

Anyhow the Gloucester vision ought to last you for years.

Don't be silly—me I mean.

Kindest regards to the Rectory

Yours sincerely

EDWARD ELGAR

On 16 October His Excellency and the Lady came to tea
with us at Wolverhampton. There was a concert that night
at Birmingham and they came to us when the rehearsal was
over. I did not go to the concert. How we talked! The Lady
and my stepmother naturally had much to say and I had much
music to hear.

I stayed in London for a few days in December and spent
the afternoon of the 13th with Nimrod at his house at Muswell
Hill. I was terribly sad and shocked at the change in him and
it was a very great effort to me to forget it and try to be amusing
and cheerful. I could not help realizing that the end was fast
approaching. Dear 'Small German' (as he used to call himself),
what a tragedy this was! Such a brilliant brain and such quick
wit and understanding of people and things, such fine enthusiasm for genius, expressing itself in a torrent of words! I had
to do my full share of the talking that day though, as talking
made him cough and it was a cough that shook him.

If I am to believe my diary I only saw the Elgars on two days
in 1908 and had not a single letter from His Excellency. I had
an Easter card from Rome where they were for a few weeks.

On 3 April I had a letter from Nimrod. After saying how
ill he had been he cheered up a little:

Plâs Gwyn

One of the letters I did manage to write was to Elgar who sent me the proofs of his five new part-songs, which I suppose you have seen by now? They are splendid, are they not? The first one, 'There is sweet music here' is an exquisite conception, a perfect Gem, a masterpiece worthy of E. at his best. . . .

I wrote Ivor Atkins a card the other day asking about his programme for the (Worcester) Festival. He wants to do Debussy's 'Après-midi d'un faune'! Oh! if the 50,000,000 Worcester parsons knew the lewd, impossible <u>poem</u> on which this music is built! There would be an outcry and a show of Holy Horror! Debussy is a thorough Décadent &, well—he must be a pig to choose such a poem to be inspired. Music is coming to a fine pass to need such crutches to keep it going. All the same I like the piece—as music —very much.

I say, what <u>is</u> Elgar composing now? You, as Keeper of the Archives <u>must</u> know, surely. He never tells me now, the wretch. I am glad you are coming to London soon. Ja! I <u>do</u> hope you will come and see me. I will try if the weather will let me—to get a little stronger by then & so we can have a long chat.

Ta Ta. Very sincerely yours

A. J. JAEGER

I went to Ireland in August 1908 for a month and returned just in time for the Worcester Festival. I went down on the Thursday and lunched, in the interval, with the Elgars. I heard all about the Symphony being finished and ready for the production in Manchester on 3 December and that it was to be done at the Queen's Hall and at Hereford soon after.

I could not go to any of these performances, alas! but I was delighted to hear from Nimrod that he had been at the Queen's Hall, having been 'fetched, by a kind friend, in a motor cab all the way from Muswell Hill'. He wrote:

How I wish you had been there. I never in all my experience saw the like. The Hall was packed; any amount of musicians. I saw Parry, Stanford, E. German, J. Corder, E. Faning, P. Pitt, E. Kreuz, etc. The atmosphere was electric. . . . After the first movement E. E. was called out; again, several times, after the third, and then came the great moment. After that superb Coda (Finale) the audience seemed to rise at E. when he appeared. I never heard such frantic applause after any novelty nor such shouting. Five times he had to appear before they were pacified. People stood up and even on their seats to get a view. As regards my impressions, I must say I was delighted. The lovely Heavenly Adagio reduced me to tears. The Scherzo both amused and charmed me. The Coda is superb and winds up the symphony in a blaze of glory. That Coda is quite new in laying out and effect. On the whole a splendid & noble & highly individual work, full of the most lovely detail work & any amount of Brains & Heart. . . .

I went on Saturday too & took my wife & we enjoyed the work immensely. The House was packed again, & Busby, the managing Director of the Symph: Orch: Co. told me the day was a record for them in the way of selling tickets. . . .

Yours

NIMROD

On 9 December I went down to Worcester for a concert at which the Brodsky Quartet was playing. I did not keep the programme and I cannot remember anything about the afternoon except that I had tea with the Elgars and the usual party of friends afterwards, and that I met Dr. G. R. Sinclair for the first time. He and I travelled back as far as Birmingham together—he was Conductor of the Birmingham Festival Choral Society and was due there that evening for a rehearsal.

We talked of many things, including music, and bulldogs! I had heard of Dan and of his fall into the Wye and we speculated as to whether he was the only dog immortalized in music. I heard of his devotion to, and unwillingness to leave, his master, and that he was a regular attendant at the Hereford Choral rehearsals.

'What does he do while you are taking rehearsals?' I asked.

'He lies under my desk and sometimes gets kicked by accident, but he does not seem to mind. The thing he cannot stand is people singing out of tune; then he growls. Once the tenors sang so flat that I had to turn Dan out.'

'*What* a reflection! Fancy being told you sing flat enough to turn a dog out! I'm thankful it wasn't the sopranos, anyway.'

Birmingham was reached all too soon and we went our several ways, he to his rehearsal and I to continue my journey home. Thus I made another 'Variation' friendship.

The Elgars spent Christmas 1908 at home and on 7 January 1909 I went to Hereford for a couple of days.

I had been to hear the Symphony at the Queen's Hall on 1 January with two friends, and I went with them to their home in Rochester for a week, and then on to Hereford. That first evening at Plâs Gwyn we had much to say about the Symphony: the splendid performances: three since the production at Manchester on 3 December! I told them how delighted dear Nimrod was with it and how he had written me a huge long letter all about it. I thought they both looked very grave and the Lady changed the subject very quickly. Afterwards I heard that they had both been so dreadfully shocked and grieved to see such a change in him that it had rather upset them. I don't wonder. It is really amazing that he managed to go to Queen's Hall, even by 'motor cab', and enjoy it.

'I am sure it was an immense pleasure to him to be there,' I said, 'and he can have so few pleasures now.'

I think it was about the year 1909 that E. E. began to find his presence more and more necessary at London meetings and engagements generally and the constant journeys became very tedious and a great waste of time. He used to come back so tired and bored that he was disinclined to settle down to the accumulations of work at home.

There was one particular occasion of which I am thinking. When I arrived on a visit I was told how much work there was waiting to be done and how he had 'been so naughty' and would not attend to it. Letters to be written and proofs to be corrected and all sorts of things—'and he hasn't touched the piano for days. Oh, *dear* Dora! You *will* try your best, won't you, to cheer him up? Perhaps he will attend to those proofs— they ought to have gone back *days* ago!'

At dinner he was silent and rather grumpy; I did most of

the talking. I told them about amusing things that had happened at home lately, funny things at Choral Practices under Henry J. Wood, everything that I could think of that might interest or amuse. Towards the end of dinner I did succeed in making him laugh and the Lady looked positively grateful.

After dinner we had coffee in the study and when we had all finished she sat back on the sofa looking nearly done to the world, remarking:

'Shall you think it *very* rude, dear Dora, if I slipped off to bed now? I am so *very* tired!'

He opened the door for her and went upstairs with her. Waiting for him to come down again, I remember feeling a little nervous; so much seemed to be expected of me. Should I succeed again as I had before? But nervousness would be hopeless and would wreck everything. It was an honour to feel oneself accounted one of the family, able to take a turn and be a help.

It often used to take a long time and a great deal of patience before the mood arrived when he felt inclined to touch the subject of music. Of course I never mentioned the word, or work of any sort. I just listened and sympathized and laid myself out to be amusing and a distraction from worry generally.

Sooner or later—and on this particular occasion it was much later—the time would arrive, sometimes with surprising suddenness:

'Come on, let's do some music,' and we were soon deep in it—I turning over—first one thing and then another. On and on we went, forgetting the time. He seemed to have shaken off the depression like a sort of cloak and to be like his old self again. I remember I heard a lot of music that night, both old and new, and finally the first movement of the E flat Symphony.

'Where are those proofs? Oh, there they are—that's my morning's work to-morrow.'

I looked at the clock.

'*This* morning's work you mean.'

82

'My giddy aunt! Look at the time! Cut along, child, I *shall* catch it.'

As I went slowly upstairs I realized that I was dead tired, but what a triumph it was. I had done it again.

That morning, at breakfast, before E. E. appeared, the Lady told me that she had lain 'awake for an age, it seemed; and then at last I heard the piano! Oh, I *was* so glad and thankful! and I went to sleep quite soon after that.'

Poor little dear! One can so easily understand how the anxiety and worry of it all would get on her nerves. Letters unanswered and promises &c. unfulfilled, and even the possibility that contracts might be broken; it must have been very worrying for her.

It was easy enough for me to be light-hearted with no background of anxiety.

On 24 April there was a very fine performance of *Gerontius* at Queen's Hall to which I took five friends. I think only one of them had ever heard it before, so it was rather an occasion.

The Elgars went to Italy early in May and I had a card from him at Careggi, Florence, dated 4 May 1909.

On 19 May I had a letter from Mrs. Jaeger telling me of her husband's death and giving me his 'Goodbye' message. So it had come at last, and Nimrod had passed on. There were obituary notices on A. J. Jaeger in nearly every paper that had any interest in music. I remember one critic spoke of him as 'one of the quickening forces in the music of his day'.

His passing was a great grief and loss to Elgar and he felt it acutely. Not only was Nimrod a dear friend, but Elgar attached great weight to his genial and outspoken criticisms.

It was when I went down to Hereford in August 1909 that I found another person installed at Plâs Gwyn—a turtle-dove. It had a large wicker cage in the veranda, but the door was always open and the dove came and went as it liked.

I remember well, arriving after an exceedingly hot and dusty railway journey. The house felt beautifully cool and there were flowers everywhere. I came downstairs after a welcome wash and change and I saw that the study door was ajar. Pushing it open a little I just caught sight of a vision and though I instantly 'froze' I was too late, the dove had seen me and was gone. E. E., in a linen coat, with a pinky-coloured tie, was at his writing-table and the dove had been sitting on the stationery cabinet in front of him. His Excellency looked up and saw me.

'There you are. Did you see Dove? I wish she wouldn't sit there. She sits and watches my pen every time I want more ink. I know she'll put her beak in the inkpot one day.'

'New and interesting variety of dove,' I remarked. 'The inky-beaked turtle-dove.'

'Look here, I'm trying to write a letter. I can't think how you expect me to write sense.'

'I never expect——' There was Dove on the window-sill! Would she come back? Standing motionless by the table looking at some music seemed to be a reassuring attitude in a stranger, and in she came. She perched on the pole of the library steps and sat there looking at me, first with one eye and then with the other.

'If you'd stay a decent time and not flit as you always do she'd soon be all right,' E. E. said very quietly.

'Well,' I said unwisely, 'I'm staying three whole days this time.'

'There's Alice ringing the bell for tea and I've not finished this writing. If only Alice wouldn't ask visitors whom one doesn't want—O my unhappy gizzard! *Do* go away—Dove's gone long ago.'

Tea was set out under the great cedar on the lawn and there was the Lady, looking lovely and cool in a blue frock, arranging comfortable chairs. The garden was gay with flowers and the veranda was half-smothered with climbing roses. Butterflies danced along the borders in the sunshine, and close to us,

SIR EDWARD ELGAR

*Taken in 1909 by Miss May Grafton at Plâs Gwyn,
Hereford*

in the cedar, sat the Dove. She had much to say, and after tea we sat silent; it was all so lovely.

Then I heard more about the Dove.

'She led me a fine dance in the spring,' E. E. said. 'I thought she seemed out of sorts, but I did not guess at once what was the matter. She used to wait till I was near the cage and then go into it and sit down on the floor. I believe she wants to make a nest! I said to myself; well, why doesn't she do it? Next day I found her in the veranda struggling with a great stiff straw. She flew up with it over and over again trying to get in through the cage-door. At last she got it in and proceeded to sit down on it in a helpless sort of way and she looked at me with such a reproachful expression! I wondered what she wanted me to do. "You absurd thing," I said, "you can't expect me to show you how to make a nest?" But evidently she did; so I went round the place looking for things—feathers, bits of hay, leaves —Dove watching me all the while and never very far away. Of course I didn't trouble to arrange the stuff, I just put it down in a little heap on the floor of the cage and thought she'd use the nesting-box, but not a bit of it! There she was next morning, sitting on it just as I'd put it—and she'd laid an egg! No, there were no bung yirds! Dove was a bad sitter; pity, wasn't it?'

That evening we watered the garden (E. E. was quite good with a hose) and then we sat out until it was nearly dark. We visited Dove, who had long ago retired for the night, and then we settled down to music.

The windows were wide open and the curtains drawn back, and lovely scents came in from the garden. I think I must have heard most of the sketches for the Violin Concerto that evening, and how I loved it, every bit of it, from the beginning.

(A year later I heard the revised Concerto, played all through to me from a printed proof copy, and I thought I had never heard anything more beautiful. What sadness and regrets, what high hopes and dreams was he describing? Alone in the study, just before leaving for home, I found the copy on the table and turned at once to pages which I had not noticed while I was busy with turning over. Having examined the title-page I came next to the Spanish quotation on a page by itself. I knew no Spanish, but the word 'alma' struck me—was it not 'soul'? —and then the blank space with five dots caught my eye and a name immediately sprang to my mind. The door opened and the Lady came in. She came and stood by me, saw what I was looking at, and translated the Spanish sentence: 'Herein is enshrined the soul of . . . . .' Then she went on to fill in the name—that of a personal friend—and asked me never to reveal it. I promised her that I never would. My guess was right.

I think it may be conceded that there must be, in practice, a time-limit to the value of such a promise as the one I gave to Lady Elgar in 1910.

Writing as I do now, in 1946, I feel that the limit in this case has been reached. Carice Elgar-Blake agrees with me and it is with her full consent that I make known that the five dots in the Spanish quotation have concealed the identity of Mrs. Julia H. Worthington, a most charming and kind American friend. She was known to intimate friends by another name—also of five letters, and I cannot say definitely whether the composer had this name or her first Christian name in mind. Nor does this matter; the gap is now filled.

Next day and the day after were both gloriously hot. We breakfasted out on the lawn under the cedar, in fact we had all our meals out, closely attended by Dove. His Excellency was busy and worked indoors the first morning, and I wrote letters at the table under the cedar. Dove was rather worried about it. She sat near me for a bit and then flew over to the house and I saw her disappear through the study window. She would be there for a short while and then come back again to me; in fact, she spent the whole morning going to and fro. How I wished I could understand what she was saying as she bowed and curtsied. She *was* a darling!

Next day a batch of proofs came from Novello's and I unpacked them. It seemed so dreadful to have no exuberant letter from dear Nimrod and I spoke of it.

'Don't talk about it. It's too sad. I can't bear it.'

But that evening, sitting in the study—the Lady having said 'Good-night' early and departed to bed—we talked much about him. I told E. E. how I had spent the whole afternoon at Muswell Hill the previous winter; how I had tried my utmost to cheer him, and how I had cried most of the way home in the train afterwards.

During this visit to Hereford I was taken to see the 'Ark',[1] as the beautifully fitted-up little laboratory at Plâs Gwyn was called. I went round reading the names on the bottles and came to a part of a shelf which had empty bottles, but with named labels.

'What have you done with the stuff out of these bottles?'

'There's been no "stuff", as you call it, in them; they are ready for the stuff when I make it.'

'Oh, *do* make one now and let me help.'

So he made up one of the things and I waited on him and brought what he asked for.

'If you were my regular assistant', he remarked, 'you'd have to be quicker.'

'If you'd ask for things by the names on the bottles I should do better,' I retorted.

So we wrangled playfully on and the finished product was at last made and duly housed in its bottle and put back into place.

'There,' he remarked, 'we've made up one more. But it is far more exciting to make something absolutely new. Look at this,' taking down a bottle from a different shelf, 'here is something I've created myself, and it's going to be called after me.'

'That's splendid!' I said—and I just bit my tongue in time —I was on the point of adding, 'What's it *for*?' which would have been a fatal remark.

[1] It was rather like a toy Noah's Ark from the outside.

I have learned more recently that E. E. found this work really engrossing and that often he was doing chemistry in the Ark when important music matters were awaiting his attention indoors, and it was difficult to persuade him to leave the one and attend to the other.

The Elgars had rather a hectic time of it at the ensuing Three Choirs Festival at Hereford. They were looking forward to having a jolly house-party for it at Plâs Gwyn, but Carice upset all their plans by developing scarlet fever. Nothing daunted, however, they took Harley House, in Hereford, and had their party there. The story of what happened about the lack of bells is vividly described by Mr. W. H. Reed in his book, *Elgar as I knew him*. The bedrooms at Harley House were not fitted with bells and E. E. raided a Hereford toy-shop for all sorts of things that would make a noise and these were hung up outside the doors. I should think there were no straight faces among the domestic staff during that Festival.

The Birmingham Festival (1909) was in October, and on the Tuesday evening we had a fine performance of the Symphony and on the Wednesday morning we had *Gerontius*—both conducted by Hans Richter. Birmingham really heard *The Dream* this time. I saw His Excellency at both concerts, but did not speak to him.

On 25 November I went to Oxford to stay with Mr. and Mrs. R. B. Townshend. There was an orchestral concert at which the *Variations* were to be done and R. B. T. wanted to go to it with me. Poor thing! I'm afraid he was rather bored —he was entirely unmusical—but he was entertained by what I could tell him of the other 'Variations' and amused by my 'explanatory notes' on the subject of his brother-in-law, 'W. M. B.'.

'E. E. called you the "Delight-maker", didn't he?'

'Yes; that was after those theatricals when I did the old man. Those *were* the days!'

He wanted to know why W. M. B. was amused and why he said what he did at Worcester after the 'R. B. T.' Variation, and in what way I thought it was like him. This was a little awkward for me as I could not very well tell him how wickedly like him it was, with all his funny little eccentricities and ways of speaking. However, I told him what I could.

'That's no end interesting,' he said, 'but I wish I could see it just as you do!'

I do not appear to have had a Christmas-card from either E. E. or the Lady, but I received a crazy letter from him dated 7 January 1910. He seemed to have been in a very good humour when he wrote. On the back of the envelope was his new seal, not, this time, of home manufacture.

On 24 January I went up to London for the Jaeger Memorial Concert at the Queen's Hall. I found it rather a trying experience, particularly the *Variations*. I noticed, however, that others found it 'trying' besides myself. I was glad to see that the Hall was well filled and I wondered, looking round before the concert began, how many of those present had really known him personally. It was a fine tribute to the memory of the great 'Small German' who had done so much for English music.

In the following April I went abroad—to Florence this time. The evening before I started[1] I dined with the Elgars at 58 New Cavendish Street, the flat they took from Mrs. Strong. I had a delightful evening, hearing all the news and also hearing a good deal of the E flat Symphony which was to be produced in the following year. I remember that I had various passages from the second movement singing in my head for days after.

I had a wonderful time in Florence, but it ended tragically. At breakfast, in my hotel, on 8 May, the nice elderly waiter who

[1] Monday, 11 April.

89

had taken charge of me and my meals all the while I had been there made his way over to my table obviously much concerned about something. 'Signorina,' he said, in a very low voice, 'il vostro Re è morto!' It made one feel as though one was at the Antipodes—I don't quite know why. The few other English people and I looked our grief and concern at one another and waited for further news. Next day I left for England and found myself a conspicuous object, in colours, when I landed; but I arrived home that evening decently clad.

Carice Elgar came to stay with us at Wolverhampton in July for our great annual Floral Fête. I think she enjoyed the flowers, the bands, and the fireworks as much as any of us.

The following week E. E. went up to York for the Festival and met Professor Granville Bantock there. The Queen's Hall and the Northern Orchestra (led by Rawdon Briggs) was under the conductorship of Mr. T. Tertius Noble, organist at York Minster. The soloists were Agnes Nicholls, Phyllis Lett, Gervase Elwes, and Herbert Brown.

At the opening concert there was a selection of Elgar works including the *Sea Pictures* and the *Enigma Variations* 'very finely played', and Granville Bantock's *Song of the Genie* 'sung with great effect by Herbert Brown'.

King Olaf was the chief work at the final concert, and a first performance was given of Bantock's *Suite of Dramatic Dances* 'which displayed Professor Bantock's elegant and delicate fancy in orchestration, to great advantage'. The two composers conducted their own works at both concerts.

During the week the two friends went sight-seeing round the City. Sir Granville Bantock writes,

The portrait of Elgar and myself was taken during the Musical Festival . . . and appeared later as a picture postcard . . . the idea originally occurred to Elgar as we were strolling through the streets of York during a free afternoon.

I found the postcard, on sale in Birmingham, later that year.

AT THE YORK FESTIVAL, 1910

Plâs Gwyn

In August that year (1910) we all went away on our usual summer holiday and Saturday morning, 3 September, found me on my way to stay with Miss Danks at Gloucester for the Festival. I had heard from the Lady that they were taking a house on College Green, known as the Cookery School, for the week, and I was asked to bring Amy Danks to tea with them there on that Saturday. We got there early and I heard that several people were expected to tea besides the house-party, so there were lots of things that I could do to help the Lady.

Unusual noises were coming from somewhere upstairs and the Lady told me that Herr Kreisler and E. E. were going through the Violin Concerto behind locked doors! Having done all I could for the moment downstairs I went to look for Amy.

'Look here, I'm not going to miss all this. What about you?'

So we both slipped away upstairs and sat on the top step outside the door. It *was* interesting! Kreisler was trying bit after bit—not playing it properly, of course—but he was getting the composer's meaning and ideas. They did not speak one another's language very well and it was difficult at times. Kreisler became worried and anxious now and again and then at last he understood and raced off with it joyously. Loud applause from the piano. At last we tore ourselves away. Tea was coming in and the Lady might want me. There were a good many people there and we sat down to a long table.

'Will you sit at the end, dear Dora, and then when H. E. and Herr Kreisler come down perhaps you could stay and look after them if we've all done?'

That quite fitted in with my ideas, but we were hardly more than half-way through tea before the door opened and they came in. E. E. was in high spirits and demanded much tea, and I was introduced to Herr Kreisler and waited on them both. I do not know what the latter thought of it, or how much he understood of it, but he smiled when we laughed and I laughed so much I could hardly finish my tea.

'Did you see about the farewell to the missionaries, in the local paper, Dorabella?'

'No,' I said, putting down my cup for safety's sake. 'What happened?'

'Well, the paper said a party of them were being seen off at Foregate Street station and a large crow on the platform sang a hymn.'

That seemed to please E. E. immensely.

Tea was finished at last and soon afterwards Amy and I left.

'Come to-morrow evening at about 9 o'clock, dear Dora, will you? and bring Miss Danks.' Then the Lady added mysteriously: 'There's going to be something *quite interesting*!' But no more would she say and we speculated all the way home as to what it might be.

The opening service of the Festival was on Sunday afternoon and was hugely attended as it always is. Professor Sanford Terry, whom I had met at tea at the Elgars' the previous day, was one of the stewards.

The evening came at last.

'Let's be in good time,' I said. 'They won't mind, and you never know!'

But, early as we were, we heard a buzz of voices as we reached the door and the hall seemed to be nearly full of people already —mostly men, I noticed.

What *was* going to happen?

The piano that had been upstairs on the Saturday was now in the hall near a window, and a light was cleverly arranged near it; there was a music-stand by the piano and I saw Mr. W. H. Reed.

'It's the Violin Concerto!' I said to Amy Danks as we wormed our way to where the Lady was dispensing coffee.

'Dear Dora,' she said, 'you and Miss Danks must please pack yourselves away in a very small space, there are many more coming than I expected and I'm *very* doubtful about the chairs!'

So we wedged ourselves into one of the two window-seats and were pretty close to the piano.

'My dear, *do* look at the pictures!'

Amy Danks, being herself an artist, had noticed before I had that all the pictures were turned round facing the wall. Some of them were draped with material and some were not.

'Isn't it too comic?' I said. 'I've known them do that elsewhere. I always want to go and peep behind to find out what they are.'

People were beginning to settle themselves now. I saw Professor Terry, Mr. Schuster, Dr. Brewer, Mr. Ivor Atkins, and Mr. Lee Williams among those present. It was a very warm evening; every door and window was open. People sat about all over the place, on the arms of chairs, up the stairs, and on the floor. 'No one minds if I play in my shirt-sleeves, I suppose,' said E. E., taking off his coat. 'You know I can't play this stuff.'

Then, to Mr. Atkins: 'You come and play the treble and I'll play the bass.'

Just before they began E. E. said in a low voice to Mr. Reed: 'You won't leave me alone in the tuttis, will you?'

I was half-afraid that E. E. might indulge in his curious habit of 'singing' while he was playing. It was an odd noise: it seemed to be a kind of filling in of parts that he had not fingers enough to play. It was really more like grunting than singing. He actually did do it at the start, but whether it was that one became so absorbed, or whether he stopped doing it as anxiety lessened, I do not know. Nothing, however, spoilt the beauty of the performance. Mr. Reed evidently knew the Concerto inside out and played it splendidly. It really was glorious! And there were we among this select and privileged audience hearing it for the first time.

On the way back Amy Danks and I discussed ways and means for being together at the production in London in November.

The next day was filled with rehearsals in the Cathedral and I first met Mrs. Worthington, one of the many friends that the Elgars had made in the States, and I sat next her during the whole of the morning. Unfortunately none of E. E.'s music was rehearsed. I did so want to find out how much she knew of it and what her feelings about it were; but we had no opportunity of talking and, so far as I can remember, though I saw her every day during the Festival and we nodded and smiled to one another, I hardly spoke to her again.

On Friday morning it was *Messiah*. Professor Terry promised to take me up into the Triforium of the Choir for it—the Elgars usually heard it from up there—and as soon as the doors were shut and his duties as steward were over, I followed him up. At the top of the steps there was a flat space, rather gloomy and dark, and there was His Excellency, lying full length on three chairs, his head on a large red cushion, with arms folded over his chest and eyes shut. He heard our steps, and when he saw me he made an awful face and pointed with his thumb to the other side of the Triforium and shut his eyes again. Professor Terry and I went round to the north side where we found the Lady and Mrs. Worthington already established. We heard most beautifully, everything, words and all (though knowing it almost by heart helps a good deal), but it must be remembered that all the singers had their backs to us—another testimonial, if one were needed, to the extraordinary merits of Gloucester Cathedral acoustically. It came through to us better than I could have imagined possible. And what a blessing it was to see no audience and no soloists and no mannerisms! One just heard the music without any hindrances. No wonder that E. E. chose that part of the Cathedral.

On 10 November 1910 Amy Danks and I went together, as we had planned, to the Queen's Hall to hear the production of the Violin Concerto. The place was simply packed. Kreisler came on looking as white as a sheet—even for a player of his great experience it must have been a nervous moment—but he played superbly. E. E. was also, obviously, very much strung up; but all went well and the ovation at the end was tremendous. Kreisler and E. E. shook hands for quite a long while and they returned to bow their acknowledgements I don't know how often. Finally they came in arm-in-arm.

I used to think that I would always rather hear Kreisler play the Elgar Concerto than anyone else. His wonderful mastery, tone, and absence of sentimentality are most refreshing. His reading of the Cadenza is unique.

But there was another master fiddler whom Kreisler heard play this concerto at a rehearsal and whose admiration of it drew from him spontaneous praise: Eugen Ysaÿe. There is an account of this in Vladimir Cernikoff's book, *Humour and Harmony*.

Cernikoff writes:

... Since that day, whenever I had the opportunity I rushed to hear Ysaÿe, and during the time I was in Germany I frequently travelled a few hours for the privilege of hearing that supreme artist. One of the most interesting and unforgettable occasions was a rehearsal at the Philharmonic Concert Hall in Berlin of Elgar's concerto. He had a way of playing the Cadenza in that very beautiful work in such a detached manner that for once, the expression 'Music from Heaven' seemed inadequate. Behind me were seated Fritz Kreisler, Mischa Elman, and many other violinists of fame. I remember the terms of profound enthusiasm in which Kreisler spoke to his wife about the performance.

It is a great pity that England never heard one of the greatest masters that ever lived play this concerto. I am quite aware that there were difficulties, but it is surely a thousand pities that those difficulties were found to be insuperable and that no bridge of agreement could have been constructed. It is a great loss to English music, and as I am given to understand that Ysaÿe made no gramophone record the loss is even more complete. Those who remember the sumptuous tone that Ysaÿe got out of his violin—particularly on the G string—can *you* picture the solo violin's first entry? It has always seemed to me that the solo instrument has been playing in another world and decides at last, nearly at the end of a phrase, to make itself heard in this one.

But it is of the Cadenza that Kreisler spoke most highly—he, who plays it so superbly himself.

What must it have been like?

I do not seem to have heard anything of the Elgars all that winter—not even a Christmas-card—but on 27 March 1911 I had a card from him posted at Queenstown with a picture of a Cunard liner and the one word 'Goodbye'. He was off again to the States; this time, alone. I do not know how long he stayed there, but he was back in England for the London Musical Festival which took place at the end of May.

Sir Henry J. Wood conducted the Violin Concerto on the 23rd with Kreisler as soloist, and the Second Symphony was produced on the 24th, conducted by the composer. That was another great success and E. E. got a fine ovation.

I wrote, as usual, for his birthday on 2 June and received the following reply:

75 Gloucester Place
Portman Square. W.

My dear Child ('m, 'm!)   June 7, 1911

We are just back from the country where we successfully avoided
Music
Church
Noise
Heat & other disagreeables & got stung many times instead.

Thank you for your infantile prattle which was most inopportune—why remind me of my birthday?

(Mistaken wretch!)

This lovely phrase is what Hercules says in Handel's work to 'Pleasure' who invites him to the Dance, etc.

I like it: 'Mistaken wretch'—yes! it's good and not too poetic.

Mistaken wretch!

It is hot: butter melts in the shade, also ice.

When are you coming? we are here for some time longer.

My love to all: but you should not remind me of my birthday: respeck the aged.

Mistaken wretch!

Yours disjointedly

The fifth letter: unless you count backwards.

P.S. The sanity of the writer (not of the writee) can be guaranteed for a small fee. If the receiver doubts the accuracy of the mess (!) age it can be repeated at half rates.

Among the Honours conferred at the Coronation of King George V (22 June 1911) appeared

SIR EDWARD ELGAR, *Order of Merit.*

'THE O. M.'

I HAD been a good deal laughed at at home for my championship of Elgar. I am afraid that they accused me of an admiration for his music to the exclusion of all other composers. This was hardly fair and the accusation was quite unjustified. Anyhow, E. E. was always alluded to as 'The Only Composer'! It was not until the Coronation Honours were published in June 1911 that this title was abandoned for another: 'The O. M.' now took its place.

The Elgars left Hereford early in the New Year and went to live at Hampstead. I had a card from Professor Sanford Terry dated 22 January 1912, which ended:

The E's are settling into 42. Netherhall Gardens. I lit the first fire in the Dining Room 10 days ago! He is very happy and working at the Masque.[1] C. S. T.

Severn House (as they called their new home) had a very large and beautifully panelled studio which made a magnificent music-room. Off this large room opened a small one, partly lined with bookshelves, which he used as a study.

'You *are* in clover here,' I said, 'and fancy having a study as well!'

'I don't know about the clover—I've left that behind at Hereford—but Hereford is too far away from London; that's the trouble. Look here, do you see that I've got room for a billiard-table? Perhaps you'll see it the next time you come.'

I heard some of the Masque that day and also some of *The Music Makers*. After playing the passage which ends 'The singer who sings no more', he said:

'How do you like that?'

But I could not answer. Thinking of Nimrod I turned away and said presently:

---

[1] *The Crown of India.*

Histed

SIR EDWARD ELGAR: O.M.

June 1911

'That's going to be terribly trying to listen to. Bringing in "Novissima hora est" there is simply wonderful.'

I did not see them again till the Birmingham Festival the following October. On the Tuesday evening we had the production of *The Music Makers* with Muriel Foster as soloist and I have no words to describe how beautifully she sang it. Dear 'Small German'! How he would have loved it!

There was a very fine performance of *The Apostles* on the Friday evening and we saw the Lady for a few minutes afterwards. Sir Edward conducted both *Apostles* and *Music Makers*, so there was no chance of seeing him—except his back!

I lunched with them at Severn House on 12 April 1913, and he played me a good deal of *Falstaff*.

I did not see them again till we met at the Gloucester Festival. There was a fine performance of *Gerontius* on the Tuesday and the Second Symphony was on the Thursday morning.

I heard *Gerontius* for the sixteenth time at Birmingham, in October, and heard *Falstaff*, the *Variations*, and the Second Symphony at the Queen's Hall, conducted by Landon Ronald, in November.

In the spring of 1914 I paid another visit to the Elgars. I had married in the previous January, and I took my husband to see them and make their acquaintance. I kept in touch with them by being, still, Keeper of the Archives; but here my memories end.

'MY FRIENDS PICTURED WITHIN'

THE programme notes for the Richter Concert which took place at St. James's Hall, 19 June 1899, when the *Variations* were produced, contained the following:

On being asked for some elucidation of the composer's intentions, Mr. Elgar replied:

'It is true that I have sketched for their amusement and mine, the idiosyncrasies of fourteen of my friends, not necessarily musicians; but this is a personal matter and need not have been mentioned publicly.'

While I am in complete agreement with this idea one need not lose sight of the fact that years have elapsed since this music was written, and that now, in 1946, I am the only member of the circle of thirteen friends who is still living and able, not only 'to tell the tale', but to put straight some of the incorrect statements that have been made—both written and spoken—on this subject. Further, the popularity of the *Variations* to-day has naturally led to a certain amount of interest in the personalities portrayed, and in the hope of adding still further to interest already widely shown I have given some particulars concerning those whom I knew and adding a few remarks about the three whom, sad to say, I never met.

What I have set down in this chapter is in no sense biographical; I have merely stated facts as I knew them and described happenings in which I participated or which have been told to me by eye-witnesses.

From his many friends, Elgar chose the thirteen to whom he alludes as 'My Friends Pictured Within', adding himself as the fourteenth. The friends were chosen, not because he had any particularly great regard for each one, but because the thought of them gave him ideas which could be described in music. Some of them can be called portraits: C. A. E. and R. P. A.;

I

(C. A. E.)

Reginald Haines

others are more in the caricature class: R. B. T., W. M. B., and Troyte, while H. D. S-P., Ysobel, and B. G. N. are connected mainly with the instruments that they played. Nimrod, G. R. S., and the 'Romanza' are founded on incidents.

The portraits of the fourteen Variations illustrating this chapter were all taken between the years 1896 and 1903, with one exception—that of No. I, C. A. E. The collecting of these photographs took two years to complete. Carice Elgar-Blake had the lion's share of the work. Many difficulties were met with, touch having been lost with some of the subjects and also with their 'belongings'. One of the portraits, that of R. P. A., was at last run to earth in the United States. The collection was completed in June 1939 and one set hangs, framed, in the Elgar Birthplace House at Broadheath. My own set, rather more elaborately mounted, varies slightly from the one at Broadheath —as does the set reproduced here. I was given free leave to use which photographs I preferred to illustrate this chapter.

I
C. A. E.

It is hardly necessary for me to say much here about Caroline Alice Elgar. This book is almost a portrait of her in her unceasing enthusiasm, work, partisanship, and love for her genius-husband.

The photograph that I have chosen for C. A. E., seated at her writing-table,[1] seemed to me to be the best portrait to use though taken at a much later date. It is such a pleasant picture and the attitude is so characteristic. I saw her seated thus, struggling with newspaper cuttings, in the early days of our acquaintance and she seemed to me to grow hardly a day older in the passing of many years.

It has been said that C. A. E. 'helped' her husband with the composition of the *Variations*, but this is hardly correct. No doubt he found her amused and interested criticism valuable, but the idea and scheme of the *Variations* was entirely his own. The

[1] See p. 41.

account—given so often—of the evening when he came back from a walk and sat down to the piano and played 'something' and his wife asked 'What is that?' is so well known that I need not repeat it here. So far as I have been told, it is quite true. The phrase with which she ended what I might call the first episode of the 'trial run' of the composition is worth noting anew: 'Surely you are doing something that has never been done before?' That first evening only a few sketches were played: those which were thought of first. Others quickly followed during the next few days, but how they were received I never heard. What an interesting and exciting time it must have been! The whole set of *Variations* was not finished when I first heard some of it, that memorable 1st of November 1898, nor was the orchestration of any part of it begun. I heard that *that* was done with incredible speed! In a letter to me the composer wrote: 'I *have* orchestrated you well!' 'You' in the plural I am sure he meant, though I know that he was especially pleased with the finished 'Intermezzo'.

I add a little story which has been told me recently by a member of the Baker family. He writes:

It was in the summer of 1900 that the Elgars were staying with us at Hasfield. We boys were in the garden waiting for Nanty[1] to come out. He had waved to us from his bedroom window so I went indoors to meet him. In the hall I saw Mrs. Elgar, a packet of letters in her hand, the afternoon post having just come. She was going to take them upstairs but as she saw Nanty coming down, she waited and held the letters out to him.

'But I'm going out now', he said, taking them from her and, with a very Nantyish oath, he threw them down on the floor and they scattered in all directions.

'Oh, Edward, that <u>was</u> naughty!'

I picked the letters up and gave them to her. Remarking quietly 'These must be answered <u>at once</u>', she held them out to him. With a shout of ribald laughter he took them from her and went straight back, upstairs, without another word. I went out and told the boys that Nanty couldn't come just yet. We did not see him until tea time.'

[1] 'Nanty Ewart' (p. 37).

XII

(B. G. N.)

1896

II

(H. D. S-P.)

1896

II
H. D. S-P.

At a concert at the Queen's Hall in 1914 someone pointed Hew David Steuart-Powell out to me; but I never made his acquaintance. He was the pianist of the trio: Elgar, B. G. Nevison, and Steuart-Powell. I never heard them play; I fancy that the trio had ceased to meet before the era of my visits to Malvern began.

The Variation is based on a finger-loosening exercise that occupied the moments of preparation for Trio-playing, while stands were being put up and music found.

III
R. B. T.

The 'story' of the R. B. T. variation goes back to about 1895, before I had any connexion with the family. They were doing some amateur theatricals at Hasfield Court, the home of W. M. Baker, and someone was wanted to take the part of an old man. No one could be found who was really suitable so they ran in R. B. T., who was staying there, to act—much against his will. He had never taken part in anything of the sort before and, I was assured, never did so again. The difficulty was in what sort of voice should he speak? His voice sounded as though it had never broken. He spoke in a sort of high falsetto—rather a soft voice, and one which was eminently suitable for telling Negro stories of his travels and life in Colorado and for the same reason he was a capital reader of *Uncle Remus*. He decided to put on a deep bass voice for the old man's part, but he couldn't keep it up and his occasional lapses into his ordinary voice convulsed the audience!

Richard Baxter Townshend was rather an eccentric-looking person, with his brick-red, weather-beaten face, bright blue eyes, and shock of grey hair. And he rode about Oxford on a tricycle. Being slightly deaf he invented the idea of a bell which could be set to ring continuously like an alarum-clock. It was dreadful! Cycling with him one day I called out:

'Why *do* you let that bell ring all the time?'

'So that people can hear me coming. I can't hear *them*!'

I have called this variation a caricature, but it requires special explanation. R. B. T. was, by any reckoning, a very unusual person. He was a classical scholar of Cambridge, a first-class rifle shot, had been cattle rancher and gold prospector in Texas and Colorado, and had written books and stories about it. His two books, *A Tenderfoot in Colorado* and *The Tenderfoot in New Mexico*,[1] are interesting and amusing. He also wrote a novel, *Lone Pine*, which achieved the distinction of being reprinted in 1913 as a 'sevenpenny'.[2] His brother-in-law, W. M. B., called him a wild Irishman and objected strongly to the strange clothes he generally wore. He had a curious didactic manner of speaking—the first few bars of the Variation give it to you—and he had a trick of finishing up a rather tall-sounding story with an impressive 'I'm telling *you*' to convince you of the truth of it. Retailing more lurid stories of Mexican life to men friends, I have been told that R. B. T.'s blue eyes blazed with exasperation and excitement when the audience did not seem sufficiently impressed.

'Damn and blast it, man! Can't you understand what I'm telling you?' It is amusing to note what may be a suggestion of this in the four bars before No. 10 in the full score.

So this Variation can truly be called a portrait after all; Elgar has got him with his funny voice and manner—*and* the tricycle! It is all there and is just a huge joke to anyone who knew him well. No wonder that W. M. B. burst out laughing when he first heard it.

IV

W. M. B.

William Meath Baker was a small, wiry man, very quick and energetic. He had an incisive way of speaking—and of laying down the law sometimes. He was an excellent host, and the

---

[1] The Bodley Head, 1923.   [2] Messrs. Methuen & Co.

IV
(W. M. B.)

1898

III
(R. B. T.)

1903

Elgars called him 'The Squire'. He was always well turned out
and it is odd that I had to choose the photograph of him in his
new bicycling kit for the set of portraits of the 'Variations', but
it was the only one available at the right date. I used to like seeing him in the Hunt coat and knee-breeches which he usually
wore at dinner when there was a house-party at Hasfield. He
used to say that it was a good way of wearing the coats out! He
was a capital companion for a day's outing. Many a jolly day
have I spent with him climbing in Switzerland or on the Welsh
hills. We were about the same height and walked rather well
together. He was brother to my stepmother and we were
great friends. He was very good to me. I heard a good deal
of music with him, both at the Three Choirs' and the Birmingham Festivals and also at various concerts in London and
elsewhere. He took me to the Opera at Covent Garden
(Wagner only: no other was worth listening to—according
to him!) *Die Meistersinger* was his favourite—and I heard
that for the first time in his company. He also took me to
Rheingold and to a complete cycle of the *Ring* the following year.

On one of my frequent visits to Hasfield, a day that I particularly remember was when the whole party staying there was
taken over to a Point-to-Point meeting. The ladies of the party
were in the library after breakfast and we heard a quick step
coming along the hall. 'There's Bill,' someone said, 'Now we
shall get our orders for the day.' He came in, shut the door
sharply behind him, and stood against it.

'Oh, here you all are! That's all right. Now, about this
business to-day,' consulting a card in his hand, 'the Brougham
will take three, five can go in the brake—and someone will have
to drive over with me in the dog-cart.' His eye fell on me,
sitting on the floor near the large wood fire.

'Dora, will *you* come?'

'Oh *please*!' I cried joyfully. Now that really was delightful
and I knew that I was in for a jolly day.

'Well, look here,' he went on, 'we must get over to this place
by twelve sharp and I've arranged the start for eleven-fifteen.'

And he disappeared as suddenly as he had come, pulling the door to behind him with a loud clap. Just before eleven-fifteen I came down, ready. 'There you are! Splendid. Let's shove off at once without waiting for the others.'

Throughout the day everything went according to plan, and at top speed. When the 'events' had all been run we met for tea in a large tent. I remember the critical eyes that observed my muddy shoes!

Though the end of this Variation may remind those who knew the subject well of the sharp shutting of a door, the music is principally a picture of energy; of quick, decisive plan-making, and the issuing of orders.

There is a tendency in these days to take this Variation at such a pace that it becomes almost chaotic rather than energetic. The correct tempo should not be in doubt because the composer himself made a gramophone recording of the work.

V

R. P. A.

People have asked me which is my favourite Variation. Rather a silly question, but if I must make a choice I think I should say 'R. P. A.'. This is a portrait of a very charming person. Literary, interesting, and amusing, Richard Penrose Arnold was a delightful talker and he always seemed to me to be happy when he was with other people. I met him several times at Mrs. Hyde's tea-parties but the picture that remains with me is of the day when the tea-party after the Philharmonic Concert had to be held at another house because Mrs. Hyde had influenza, so R. P. A. invited us all to his.

It was a smaller house and there was rather a pack of people but he had it all beautifully arranged. Tea was in the dining-room, with the table pushed back across a corner, and his housekeeper pouring out from behind a large silver urn. I can see him now, fussing about among us all, finding chairs for

1903

VI
(Ysobel)

circa 1897

V
(R. P. A.)

those who wanted them, handing cakes and bread and butter, and every now and then one heard his funny little nervous laugh——

'*HA*-ha-ha, ha-ha-*HA*-ha-ha!'

(you can hear it plainly in the woodwind) as he went round talking first to one and then another.

A gentleman of the old school if ever there was one.

VI
YSOBEL

Isabel Fitton was a member of a well-known Worcestershire family, all interested in music and supporters of it. Her mother, who played the piano very well and was a brilliant sight-reader, was a great friend of my stepmother. I met many members of the family but I knew Isabel the best. She had been having some coaching in viola-playing from E. E., and the viola is the principal instrument in her Variation. The big intervals, besides being part of an exercise that E. E. wrote for her, suggest the idea that the subject was very tall—particularly the final one.

VII
TROYTE

I never fully understood the 'Troyte' Variation. Sir Ivor Atkins calls him 'that refreshing but highly argumentative Harrovian'. I had heard that there used to be great arguments but I had never been present. My recollection of Troyte in the early days was that he used to sit and grin with amusement but say hardly anything. And I never heard E. E. try to make him play the piano, which is supposed to be the idea contained in the 'cello and bass figure—Troyte playing with one finger of each hand.

I think I was rather shy of Arthur Troyte Griffith in those early days. We had not then much to say to one another, or perhaps we had little opportunity. It was not until some years later that I came to regard him as a friend; later still, when there were only the two of us left, we met more frequently and had many talks. It was always interesting to visit him at his home in Malvern, surrounded by his own beautiful water-colour sketches and treasures of one sort and another.

At the Worcester Three Choirs' Festival of 1938 I had a delightful time with him at the Elgar Birthplace House. We went into all the rooms and talked of many memories. I remember discussing some new book on Elgar and wondered how it was possible for people to write such dull books about so brilliant and amusing a person. I shall never forget his quiet reply.

'You must remember, they did not know him as we did.' This was, I think, almost his last word to me.

VIII

W. N.

This Variation has been called 'the personification of the English Countryside', and I like the idea. Winifred Norbury was essentially a country-woman. In former days the family lived at Sherridge, near Malvern, a beautiful old Worcestershire house among the woods, and one could well picture her there. E. E. was particularly fond of the lovely lanes not far from Sherridge and I like to think that W. N. was connected with them in his mind when he wrote the Variation. But this is only an idea—*not* a fact. On the other hand, my own view is that Variation No. VIII tells of a rather determined and persistent character, and I have always thought that there is more than a hint of this in E. E.'s portrait.

I only met Winifred Norbury a few times. She came to luncheon once or twice when I was staying with the Elgars, and I remember her merry little trilly laugh. I also met her at nearly all Mrs. Hyde's tea-parties after the Worcester Philharmonic Concerts—she was part-secretary, with Miss Hyde, of the Worcester Philharmonic, for some years.

But that is not knowing a person. I never had even a few

VIII
(W. N.)

1903

VII
(Troyte)

1902

minutes with her by ourselves, let alone a walk with her, which is so helpful in friend-making. I was inclined to be rather jealous of her because she could play the piano well enough to be of use to 'The Conductor', as she always called E. E. They used to go through a lot of his music together, he playing the violin. I was also rather envious of her as she lived so near and could be so readily helpful, whereas I lived so far away!

I usually planned my visits to Malvern to include a Philharmonic Concert, and had sometimes to depart for my train directly after the usual tea-party. One day E. E. had a buttonhole of Parma violets. He and W. N. and I were standing having tea together. He put his cup down, unpinned the violets—by that time much flagged—and pinned them on my coat.

'There you are, Child, with my blessing!'

'Well,' remarked W. N. rather severely, '*I* wouldn't accept cast-off flowers like that. I hope you'll throw them out of the window on your way home!'

'Perhaps I shall, who knows?' and presently I took my departure. I can hear someone say:

'What *did* you do with them, really?'

I had (I have it still) a little album into which I put a flower from all sorts of places where I had been and in memory of people and events. There is a flower from Birchwood, another from the British Camp and from many other places both at home and abroad. Quite a large collection; and among them is a Parma violet.

It has been suggested that Winifred Norbury and Mr. Jaeger were great friends and that that is why their two Variations are not only next one another but are connected by a single note. The things that people invent!

W. N. and Nimrod only met a time or two; their most interesting meeting was described by W. N. in one of her rare letters to me:

I only met Mr. Jaeger two or three times but found myself sitting next to him in the Slips at Covent Garden for a performance of

Tristan, and had delightful talks in the intervals. It was then that he told me that he 'had gone down on bended knee to implore Edwd. to make a better ending to the Vars.'[1]

IX

NIMROD

When I first heard the 'Nimrod' Variation played to me on the piano by the composer in 1898, I was greatly impressed by it. 'What a wonderful person that must be!' I exclaimed. About a year later I met Mr. Jaeger[2] for the first time. We made friends at once and so interesting and amusing did I find his friendship that I forgot completely that he had anything to do with the 'Nimrod' Variation.

It was not until 1903 that I began seriously to wonder what it could possibly mean. The music seemed to me to be so unlike him, with his volubility and his amusing—almost racy—turn of phrase. I was greatly puzzled. Surely this Variation could not be a portrait? I determined to find out the truth about this as soon as I saw a chance of doing so, and my chance came in August 1904, during my first visit to Plâs Gwyn, Hereford. I had taken my bicycle on a round of visits and E. E. and I, on a lovely, fine afternoon, set out for a ride. He took me to Holm Lacy and, leaving our cycles under some trees, we went down to the river Wye. It was lovely there. E. E. was in great form that day, talking and laughing about all sorts of things and here, at last, was my longed-for opportunity.

'Why did you give Mr. Jaeger such a grand and noble tune?' 'Don't you think him grand and noble? His *mind* is! But "Nimrod" isn't really a portrait; it is the story of something that happened.' Almost breathless with interest and excitement I waited for him to go on. 'I was very down in the dumps; everything seemed to be going wrong. I was feeling pretty wretched and I wrote and told him I was going to give it all up and write no more music.'

[1] See note on p. 125.
[2] August Johannes Jaeger.

X
(Dorabella)
Intermezzo

1902

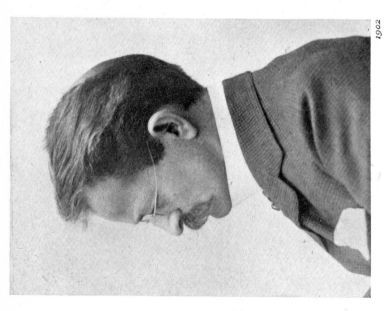

IX
(Nimrod)

1902

(I could not help smiling. I had had a letter from E. E. myself in which he said he was sick and tired of mouldy music and was going to take to kite-flying! Of course I knew he didn't mean it and that everything would be all right again soon, but one could quite imagine that a foreigner might not so easily understand.)

E. E. went on: 'He wrote me such a screed, reams and reams of it, all about my ingratitude for my great gifts, as he called them, and he abused me for my wickedness—and I don't know what else! Then he finished at last by suggesting that he should come down and talk it all over with me. Of course he came, and we went out for a long walk. Then he went at it again, hammer and tongs, and he preached me a regular sermon and sang Beethoven at me!'

'*Beethoven?*' I interrupted—

'Yes, can't you hear it at the beginning? Only a hint, not a quotation.'

(I remembered perfectly. It *had* struck me, but I wondered if E. E. had really meant it!)

E. E. went on again: 'He said that Beethoven had a lot of worries, and did *he* give it all up? No. He wrote more, and still more beautiful music—"And-that-is-what-*you*-must-do." So he won the day. It was most wonderfully good of him to have spared the time to write all that and then to come down and see me, and I am certain that he thought he had saved a critical situation by doing so.'

When E. E. had finished this story he turned to me and said gravely: 'You must *never* let him know that I have told you all this. Now promise me, Dorabella,' holding up a commanding finger.

Naturally I promised, and well have I kept my promise. I have told nobody a word about it until I began to think of writing this.

That night my mind was full of all that I had heard and of the 'Nimrod' Variation. The serenity of the Beethoven air (Adagio, Sonata in C minor, op. 13) riding triumphant over sordid worries. Then I saw Nimrod's enthusiasm and admiration for E. E. and his work, and then, in a sort of blaze of sunlight, comes the composer's regard for Nimrod, the nobility of his character, and his selfless work for the success of others. Finally, in the sudden *piano*, may one see the composer's love for his friend?

X
(DORABELLA)
Intermezzo

What I thought of this composition when I first heard it on the piano and also when I first heard it on the orchestra will be found earlier in this book. I had no idea what it really meant. It was not until many years afterwards that it dawned on me that I had been as much the victim of E. E.'s impish humour as had R. B. T. I stammered rather badly at times when I was young and as is the case with so many of those so afflicted it was a terrible trial to me. Now, I am thankful to say, that this is to a certain extent a thing of the past. Elgar exploited his humour at my expense with such marvellous delicacy that no one could help laughing with him—if they understood it. Anyhow, I have the satisfaction of knowing that nothing like the 'Intermezzo' has ever been written before or since.

All sorts of curious things have been said about it. One critic said that the 'Intermezzo' was quite out of place in the *Variations* and should have been in the *Wand of Youth*; and that (as though Elgar had lost a golden opportunity) the 'Intermezzo' had all that was required for a first-class pretty piece!

XI
G. R. S.[1]

When the *Variations* first appeared people said of this one: 'G. R. S.? Oh, of course! That's Dr. Sinclair of Hereford Cathedral, and there he is playing a pedal passage on the

[1] George Robertson Sinclair.

PERCY HULL   MAX MOSSELL
G. R. S. *and* DAN   EDWARD ELGAR

In Dr. Sinclair's garden, Hereford. 1896

organ!' Whereas some of us knew that it really was the story of what happened one day when two men went out for a walk with the dog.

Quite recently I had a letter from Dr. Percy Hull, the present organist at Hereford, and he sent me a copy of the group which is reproduced here.

Dr. Hull writes:

> Broomy Hill
> Hereford
> 13 June 1944

Dear Mrs. Powell

The enclosed rather mouldy photograph may amuse you as it shows the original No. 11 variation, i.e. G. R. S. and the bulldog Dan who is really the variation in spite of the many different versions given on the wireless and in other chit-chats! The facts are these:—About 1896, Elgar began the first of his many visits to Sinclair's house in Hereford and he always signed the Visitors' Book with a musical quotation called 'The moods of Dan'. There was 'Dan wistful', 'Dan thoughtful', 'Dan frolicsome', etc. The dog was a fine swimmer and G. R. S. used to take him to the Wye after Evensong and throw a huge chunk of wood into the water. The dog then rushed about the bank (witness bar 1) and plunged in, paddling after the stick (bars 3 and 4); this paddling passage leads to the fierce growl of joy (bar 5, double thirds) as he seized the stick, and the growls continued after he had landed. This double third passage (bar 5) was quoted in 'Moods of Dan' long before the Variations were written and it was also used in 'King Olaf' between the letters O and P in the accompaniment to the words 'they found the watch-dog in the yard'. King Olaf was first produced in 1896 and the Enigma not until 1899. By the way, the 'Dan' figure is not in the vocal score but it is definitely in the full score and is played by the violas (I speak from memory, not having seen a score for about 15 years!)

Speaking of the photograph he sends me, Dr. Hull goes on:

Note E. E.'s 'squire-leggings'! Behind the composer is Max Mossel and behind G. R. S. is your humble servant. The photograph was taken in Sinclair's garden and I only came across it the other day when turning out papers for salvage.

It may interest you to know that I was the first person ever to play the Variations in duet form with Elgar and that was from the rough proof-sheets. My hat! how we both sweated with sheer excitement!

Yours very sincerely
PERCY C. HULL

I have the 'growl' to which Dr. Hull refers, in my vocal score of *King Olaf*. It was written in by E. E. before we went up to Hanley for the production of the work at the North Staffordshire Festival in October 1896.

As to the 'squire-leggings', I remember them very well. E. E. usually wore them in the Malvern days, unless it was hot weather. Dr. Hull's photograph reminded me at once of walks and climbs up the Hills and on the British Camp.

XII

B. G. N.

I am very sorry that I never met Basil Nevinson. I have heard how delightful he was. He was the 'cellist in the piano Trio and his instrument has full scope in Variation XII in which it sings a lovely song.

Sir Ivor Atkins writes: 'The 'cello dominates the movement all through, surging over the theme, filling up points of rest and lifting it to the most impassioned heights. Here we have the characteristic interval of the seventh *in excelsis*.'

XIII

(* * *)

Romanza

Again I have to begin with regrets. I never met Lady Mary Lygon, which disappointed me very much. When I first went

1897

XIII

(* * *)

Romanza

to stay at Forli, Malvern Link, I found that she had been there that day to luncheon, and on another occasion she was coming to tea after I had left for home. This was very irritating and I used to say that they had arranged it so on purpose.

Mary Lygon had a full share of the good looks which are a regular inheritance in her family. Everyone says how charming she was. Some writers on the subject of the *Variations* have said that No. XIII was dedicated to Lady Mary *Trefusis*, but it was not until 1905 that her marriage to Major the Hon. Henry Forbes-Trefusis took place. Elgar had been over to Madresfield Court shortly before one of my visits, to help Lady Mary with some music, and she showed him round their lovely garden. His description of it all lost nothing in the telling—for my benefit, probably.

I think it is pretty well known that Lady Mary and her brother, Lord Beauchamp, were on the point of departure for Australia when the *Variations* were being finished. The composer had written asking permission of Lady Mary to use her initials at the head of No. XIII, but as his letter was not in time to catch her before they sailed he decided to replace initials by three asterisks.

It was no sort of surprise to me to hear, years afterwards, that (* * *), which to most people stand for 'Lady Mary Lygon', stood, in the mind of the composer, for 'My sweet Mary'!

XIV
E. D. U.
Finale

What further can I say about E. D. U. when this book is all about him? When 'E. D. U.' was first played to me on the piano hilarity knew no bounds. E. E. shouted with laughter. But I had not then grasped who E. D. U. was and I remember thinking what a determined and forceful person this must be. Then something, not far from the end, caught my attention; where *had* I heard that? But I could not remember and I didn't ask. There was evidently something very funny about the whole thing. When I went to Craeg Lea for the first time in May 1899, I felt I *must* get to the bottom of this puzzle. The fact was that I had not very often heard E. E. called 'Edu'[1] by the Lady, and, also, I never visualized the name she used being spelt like that. Perhaps these things are some excuse for my stupidity! When I knew the secret of E. D. U. then I also grasped the significance of the woodwind passage before No. 73 in the full score.

This is a point in connexion with the *Variations* which has never, so far as I know, been mentioned; indeed, it may be that I am now the only person who is aware of it.

In the early days at Malvern, but not, I think, later, it was E. E.'s habit to give a certain whistle with his lips when he returned home, to announce his arrival, or, at other times, to attract the Lady's attention. This whistle runs through the first part of the No. I Variation (C. A. E.) and is used just before No. 73 in the Finale (E. D. U.).

How well I remember when I first heard C. A. E. played! It seemed so curiously *like* her and I could not see how he had conveyed the idea of a 'likeness'. I think now that the whistle had a good deal to do with it. It was so definitely connected with her: it was his call to her.

Now, in the Finale, we hear the whistle and C. A. E. comes. Together they stand at the conclusion of a merry evening. The dream fades and shows the composer alone—master-artist of his Conversation piece.

So my first impression of determination and forcefulness was right. The whole Variation shows the sense of ability, the will to use it, and the triumphant fun of succeeding. He delighted in what he had done and he knew he had done it well.

The photograph of E. D. U. was taken at Malvern on 29 September 1900, and is the best likeness of E. E., at about that date, that I have ever seen. The vitality and high good humour

[1] Pronounced as short for the French name 'Édouard'.

1900

XIV

(E. D. U.)

Finale

so clearly shown seem to me to make this portrait a suitable choice for the Elgar of the *Variations*.

•

A problem at the Three Choirs' Festival has always been the provision of a large enough Hall to accommodate the crowd that wishes to attend the Wednesday Evening Secular Concert. At the Worcester Festival of 1938 a brilliant idea occurred to Sir Ivor Atkins, and he solved the difficulty by taking the new Gaumont Picture Theatre for this Concert. Probably the largest audience that has ever been seen at a Wednesday Night Concert assembled there during this Festival. The Programme included a fine performance of the *Enigma Variations*, conducted by Sir Ivor Atkins. Troyte Griffith and I were both present.

I think it was while 'R. P. A.' was being played that an idea suddenly came into my mind: 'Mrs. Hyde's tea-parties—Heavens! *Where were we* at this moment?' The Picture Theatre had been built on a site which had become available owing to the demolition of a group of houses, one of which had belonged to Mrs. Hyde—No. 21 Foregate Street.

This idea brought the whole scene at one of those delightful parties vividly to my mind; I heard R. P. A.'s laugh, and there was Troyte with his grin of satisfaction; and that succession of little trills in 'W. N.', was it her laugh or did it remind me of the triangle that she played in the Philharmonic Orchestra? At my elbow, Nimrod, running all his words together with almost unbelievable volubility, and over there, talking to somebody, was G. R. S., very stiff and straight, holding his tea-cup as though it would 'go off' at any moment (Oh! for somewhere to put it down) and E. D. U., making jokes first with one and then another, the life and soul of the party. One seemed to see them all standing about drinking tea amid a buzz of conversation and laughter.

I was so completely carried away by this idea that the outburst of applause at the end of the *Variations* was quite startling.

How the music had brought it all back!

On the way out of the Hall I found myself beside Troyte Griffith and told him of my vision.

'That *is* a curious idea! You are quite right; we must be close to No. 21 here. Queer that I never thought of it.'

THE ENIGMA

IT is strange to think that about 45 years ago I was expecting to solve the secret of the Enigma any day. Recounting to me a conversation in 1923, Troyte Griffith wrote, in a letter dated 21 September 1937:

'When I was visiting Elgar at Kempsey I asked him "Can I have one guess? Is it God save the King?"'

' "No, of course not; but it is so well known that it is extraordinary that no one has spotted it." '

'It.' Yes; we always spoke of the hidden matter as 'it', never as tune or theme.

In November 1899, E. E. chaffed me:

'Haven't you guessed it yet? Try again.'

'Are you quite sure I know it?' 'Quite.' And on another occasion:

'Well, I'm surprised. I thought that you of all people would guess it.'

'Why me of all people?'

'That's asking questions!'

Elgar made it perfectly clear to us when the work was being written that the Enigma was concerned with a tune, and the notion that it could be anything other than a tune is relatively modern. I am sure that E. E. would not have expected *me* to guess it if it had been an idea and not a tune. I was so mixed up with tunes in those days; Choral music, Church music, and orchestral music—and then my own solo singing, scenes from opera, songs, ballads, and so on. How I went through them all in my mind, trying to think of airs written in the same tempo and rhythm as the *Enigma*, and wondering which ones I had spoken of to E. E. or which he would think were connected specially with me and my work or occupations. I almost lay awake at night thinking and puzzling, and all to no purpose whatever. It *was* annoying! And most annoying of all was one day, on a visit to Malvern, when I simply begged him to tell me what it was. I suggested all sorts of tunes trying to see if I could get a rise out of him, or even a hint, and he looked at me in a sort of half-impatient, half-exasperated way and snapped his fingers, as though waiting for me to think of the tune there and then. I always feel, on looking back to that moment, that he was on the point of telling me what it was, and then he just said:

'I shan't tell you. You must find it out for yourself.'

Critics have complained that Elgar never used the word 'tune' and that, consequently, the word 'theme', which he did use, opens the door to the conclusion that the solution is an idea and not a tune at all.

Acting upon this assumption all sorts of suggestions have been put forward;—the Line of the Malvern Hills, the Personality of the Composer, and the Chromatic Scale are among them.

But it is not only my opinion that 'it' is a tune and not an idea.

In a letter to me, Winifred Norbury wrote: 'I always consider that I know the hidden tune in the Enigma, but he said I was wrong when I told him.' And in a letter to me (28 June 1942), Carice Elgar-Blake, speaking of what she and I both knew, wrote: 'We know that there was a tune.'

I should like to finish this short chapter by quoting from Mr. R. J. Buckley's book *Edward Elgar*,[1] published in 1904, which is, I think, the first Life of the composer to be written. On page 54 he writes:

'The theme is a counterpoint on some well-known melody which is never heard.'

Mr. Buckley's evidence is important because, firstly, he was acquainted with Elgar. He wrote (page 29):

'It was in the *Black Knight* period that I first visited the composer at Forli.'

[1] *Edward Elgar*, R. J. Buckley, 1904, in the Series *Living Masters of Music*, John Lane—The Bodley Head.

Secondly, in the introduction to his book he wrote:
'Whatever this book states as a fact may be accepted as such.'
Evidently he regarded his book as having Elgar's authorization.

I wish to draw particular attention to Mr. Buckley's use of
the word *melody*. It confirms precisely what I and the other
'Variants' always knew.

But it was only in this year, 1946, that I have come to
realize how mistaken I have been about this whole subject,
in spite of having read Elgar's own note in the programme
for 19 June 1899, when the *Enigma Variations* were produced.
So far as the 'note' deals with the Enigma, here it is in full:

On being asked for some elucidation of the composer's intentions, Mr. Elgar replied:
'The Enigma I will not explain—its "dark saying" must be left
unguessed, and I warn you that the apparent connexion between the
Variations and the Theme is often of the slightest texture; further,
through and over the whole set another and larger theme "goes",
but is not played . . . So the principal Theme never appears, even as
in some late dramas—e.g., Maeterlinck's "L'Intruse" and "Les sept
Princesses"—the chief character is never on the stage.'

It will be seen that Elgar carefully divides his mystery into
two parts. The first part concerns his Original Theme, and on
this he refuses to comment. The second part concerns 'another
and larger theme' that goes 'through and over' all the Variations.

In the comparison that he makes at the end of the programme
note, he further indicates that the two mysteries are, in fact,
closely related.

I feel that it is necessary to draw particular attention to what
Elgar himself said about this matter because for the last forty
years he has been persistently misquoted by almost everyone
who has written on this subject. The two mysteries have been
telescoped into one with the result that an insuperable difficulty
has needlessly been produced.

CONCLUSION

IN this book I have tried to show what Edward Elgar was like before he rose to fame and in the early years of his success. The incidents I have described and the stories I have told are all true: I have nowhere given rein to imagination.

Various competent writers have dealt with the technical side of his art and I have left the subject of his music, as such, severely alone. But the number of those who knew him forty years ago is becoming very small indeed and that is my reason for putting together these recollections of the greatest composer this country has yet produced.

Many people seem to think that a great creative artist must be more or less eccentric and a law unto himself. To them probably the most remarkable thing about Elgar, apart from his musical ability, is that he was sane and normal. He liked and enjoyed ordinary things—fun and nonsense, games and sports, birds and beasts—and was temperate and controlled. He loved his wife and he loved his home. I have always thought that his sanity is reflected in his music which, however original, is never freakish and never morbid.

Elgar's attitude towards music was curiously unprofessional. He hated teaching music and, in general, he disliked talking about it. He always pretended that he knew nothing about it, which was often funny—and sometimes a little tiresome.

When I was turning over for him I could sometimes get answers to questions, or little comments and explanations; sometimes he smiled as he was playing as though something amused him, and I have known him laugh out loud. I tried to remember the places where he had done that hoping that he would tell me about it afterwards—it was obviously impossible to interrupt at the time—but one went so quickly from one thing to another; the moment had passed; either I forgot to ask or he pretended he didn't know or would not say. Then, occasionally when we were out together he would begin singing a bit out of some well-known sonata or symphony (if I could join in with another 'part', we used to make quite a noise), and then he would discuss the music and give me his views on it.

As may be imagined, when I arrived on a visit my greatest wish was to hear new music; but sometimes he would not touch the subject of music at all and, to gain my selfish ends, I have even resorted to guile and subtlety and gone to the length of singing a tune incorrectly on purpose.

'That's wrong. Don't you know it goes like this?'

Then of course he would play it and one thing led to another. I have heard it said that he took no interest in any music but his own. This is not the case. I have heard him play *Parsifal* and *Die Meistersinger* and many passages from Mozart, Beethoven, and Brahms. I have spoken of his playing Bach. He used to say that you should begin the day by playing a Bach fugue. I do not think he actually did it himself—perhaps it was an ideal to be aimed at. He and Mr. Atkins[1] brought out an edition of the *St. Matthew Passion* (1911). He introduced me to *Phoebus and Pan* and played most of it to me at various times. He greatly admired the orchestration of Richard Strauss and Berlioz. In the region of lighter music he had a distinct weakness for the Gilbert and Sullivan operas.

He himself had a flair for this kind of music. I remember hearing the delightful merry tunes he had written in early days for a children's operetta.

'Those *are* capital tunes,' I said; 'almost as good as Sullivan!'

'*Almost* as good? Listen to this . . . and this . . .', and he played some most infectious tunes with rollicking choruses.

'Oh, *why* don't you collaborate with somebody and write a comic opera? It would be such fun!'

'I shall have to think about it some day if serious music fails.'

Then at other times he played all sorts of amusing things; bits from this and that, old songs, nursery rhymes—altered to suit his mood or in imitation of some other composer. One day I went into the study while he was playing a tune I knew quite

[1] Now Sir Ivor Atkins.

well but to which I could not put a name, and I joined in and sang it. The end of the refrain gave me the chance to ask:

'What *is* that thing?'

'*Villikins and his Dinah*; I'm going to write a fantasia on it—the trombone has the solo here and forgets the beginning of the last line—listen!'

Then he played it through and made the last line begin with two false entries with the first two notes. With a shout of laughter he played it again.

'Do you like it? I shall do something with that one of these days.'

But, unfortunately, he never did.

On the subject of contemporary English music he was, I am afraid, not very enthusiastic. He used to say:

'All these men turn out fairly good stuff, but it is "marking time" all the while and never a step forward.'

It has, I know, been said that Elgar was inclined to take himself very seriously and that his honours weighed heavily upon him. The truth is that he was a very sensitive man and was always apt to retreat into his shell if others jarred on him; but he saw the funny side of everything too clearly to become pompous or swelled-headed. This is, I think, proved to demonstration by his letter to me dated 17 December 1913.

When next we met I referred to this letter and he said:

'Did you notice the "etc."? I suppose that stands for the rest of the alphabet!'

But it is the title of President to which he adds the crown, and he ends: 'Goodbye. Yours as above—in a firmament.'

Finally, I must pay a last tribute to those two who did so much to help Elgar and stimulate his genius—his wife and A. J. Jaeger. I think it must be clear to those who have read this short personal sketch what a devoted couple the Elgars were, but I doubt if many people know what wonders that dear little woman wrought. Her efforts on his behalf were untiring. With single-minded devotion she spent herself unceasingly to help

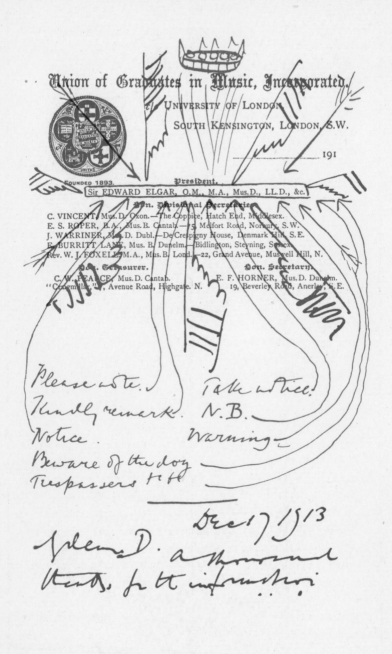

Union of Graduates in Music, Incorporated.

UNIVERSITY OF LONDON
SOUTH KENSINGTON, LONDON, S.W.

191

FOUNDED 1893. **President.**

Sir EDWARD ELGAR, O.M., M.A., Mus.D., LL.D., &c.

Hon. Divisional Secretaries.

C. VINCENT, Mus.D. Oxon.—The Coppice, Hatch End, Middlesex.
E. S. ROPER, B.A., Mus.B. Cantab.—5, Melfort Road, Norbury, S.W.
J. WARRINER, Mus.D. Dubl.—De Crespigny House, Denmark Hill, S.E.
F. BURRITT LANE, Mus.B. Dunelm.—Bidlington, Steyning, Sussex.
Rev. W. I. FOXELL, M.A., Mus.B. Lond.—22, Grand Avenue, Muswell Hill, N.

Hon. Treasurer.

C. W. PEARCE, Mus.D. Cantab.
"Craigmillar," , Avenue Road, Highgate. N.

Hon. Secretary.

E. F. HORNER, Mus.D. Dunelm.
19, Beverley Road, Anerley, S.E.

Please note.
Kindly remark.
Notice.
Beware of the dog
Trespassers + &c

Take notice.
N.B.
Warning

Dec 17 1513

[handwritten signature] D. a thousand
thanks for the information.

and encourage him. She schemed and planned, suggested and persuaded, while aiding and abetting him in all that he did. She contrived that he should meet the right people, saved him from troublesome interviews, and always did what she could to keep worries from him. She spent hours preparing orchestral score-paper and ruling bar-lines and, in addition, she did all the general secretarial work.

Often she had to be very patient. There were days when he felt disinclined for work and other times when work took possession of him and he could hardly be persuaded to stop for food or even for sleep.

In all the years I knew them I never heard anything like a cross word.

Elgar's dependence on her was such that it is small wonder to me that, after her death, he had little heart for composition.

She was indeed an ideal wife for a genius!

Mr. Jaeger was, so far as I know, the only musician with whom Elgar discussed his work in technical detail. His criticisms and advice always received the composer's careful consideration even if the suggestions were not always adopted. It was Mr. Jaeger who suggested the lengthening of the Finale of the *Variations* which led to the addition of another hundred bars.[1] I was at Malvern when the proof of the new ending

[1] By the kindness of Mr. W. McNaught (Messrs. Novello & Co.) I am able to state for the first time, I believe, the following particulars concerning dates of publication of the *Enigma Variations*:

Piano Solo, published 9 June 1899. Piano Solo, with lengthened Finale, made about September 1899. Full Score, published December 1899.

From this one learns that the first performance, on 19 June 1899, under Richter, was of the original version and was conducted from MS. Score.

The *Musical Times* of October 1899 has a column of press criticisms referring to a later performance than the first. I quote three of these:—

Daily News . . . the last movement, which has been revised.

Morning Post . . . the matter since added at the conclusion of the last Variation.

Daily Graphic. Since the first performance the composer has re-written the coda.

Mr. McNaught adds: 'The publication advertised in October (as referred

arrived and E. E. played it to me and roared with laughter, thoroughly enjoying what he had written.

'The old Moss was right,' he said.

Nimrod's own view of his work for Elgar is expressed in a letter to me dated 10 April 1907:

I have worked terribly hard for E. E. and ruined my health over it very likely. . . .

I have never loved & admired a man more, made myself more a slave for any man out of sheer enthusiasm.

to above) is piano solo, evidently with the lengthened Finale, so that the one "made in September 1899" soon got into print. The advertisement says "Full Score and Parts in the Press".'

ALTHOUGH this book deals mainly with the years 1896 to 1914, it is appropriate to refer here to the Elgar Birthplace and Museum at Broadheath, near Worcester. Opened during the Worcester Three Choirs' Festival of 1938, this cottage is now filled with memories of those early days. To look round the various treasures collected there, so beautifully and lovingly arranged, takes one back vividly to the years of his greatest creative activity. One goes from room to room noticing and remembering one thing after another:

'That picture—wasn't it in the study at Craeg Lea? And do look at that pen-tray with all the sharpened pencils! How well I remember it on his writing-table wherever he was.'

Looking at the knee-hole table a visitor would probably think how very small it was for the purpose, and he would be right. The composer wrote at a table in the centre of the room and this small writing-table was made double the size by having another table of the same height put against it. It looked like one table. This plan made room for all sorts of accessories: letter basket, ink-pots and tray, stationery cabinet, &c., with plenty of room for parcels of proof-sheets, music paper, and books. The whole of the writing-table top was thus left free. At Plâs Gwyn, in a much larger study, Elgar used a small mahogany dinner-table as his writing-table, the other one being pushed away into the bow window. It was upon this larger table that the Dove and I sometimes sat—though not together!

I once watched him orchestrating something, the 24-stave music paper held at the bottom by his left hand, the first finger at a bar on the lowest line, the right hand and pen running up to the top to do a passage for the flutes, coming down to put in something for the brass, lower for the harp, and below, a whole cascade of notes for the violins. He had forgotten me, sitting on the table close by, and I watched him—absorbed.

In the little front room at the Birthplace House where visitors sign their names in a book, stands upon a side-table a small glass case containing the Decorations and Honours presented to Elgar, including the O. M. with its bright red ribbon. I was looking at this with Carice Elgar-Blake soon after the room was arranged, and I felt puzzled.

'But didn't someone say that these were all *buried*—?'

'It *was* said, and I cannot understand how this rumour started. None of the Decorations was buried, only the red ribbon of the O. M. was buried with Mother; she loved it so, and Father wished it.[1] I shall never forget', she went on, 'the trouble we had to replace the ribbon when it was wanted for the next State occasion! And of course we had to get a new sword as well.'

But they are all there; the original Orders and Decorations, not replicas, for all to see.

There was a bowl of roses on the table; roses from the little garden which was being laid out to copy the old picture, with the row of standards on either side of the centre path. Troyte and I gave the two rose trees heading the lines, nearest to the house. Other plants for the garden were sent by intimate friends of the old days including chrysanthemums from Hasfield Court, in memory of W. M. B., and a large clump of Christmas roses came from the family of W. N.

The cottage has already become a place of pilgrimage for those who love Elgar's music, as the Visitors' Book can testify.

For me, nearly everything in it stirs memories of a wonderful friendship.

---

[1] Carice Elgar-Blake told me that buried with her Mother were, besides the ribbon of the O. M., her Father's Court Sword and the Diploma of the Institut de France.

APPENDIX

Iᴛ is well known that Elgar was always interested in puzzles, ciphers, cryptograms, and the like. The cipher here reproduced—the third letter I had from him, if indeed it is one—came to me enclosed in a letter from the Lady to my stepmother. On the back of it is written, 'Miss Penny'. It followed upon their visit to us at Wolverhampton in July 1897 (see p. 7).

I have never had the slightest idea what message it conveys; he never explained it and all attempts to solve it have failed. Should any reader of this book succeed in arriving at a solution it would interest me very much to hear of it.

September 1946.

Since the first edition of this book appeared, the cipher has, I know, been examined by a good many people skilled in such matters. Nobody, so far as I am aware, has yet succeeded in reading it.

INDEX

Æolian Harp, 64, 65
Alassio, 57
Apostles, The (libretto), 39–41, 50
First performance, 56
Birmingham (1904), 60; (1906) 75
Cologne (1904), 60; 77, 99
'Archives, the', 41–3, 63
'Ark, the' (Plâs Gwyn), 87–8
Arnold, Richard Penrose, 106–7
Atkins, Sir Ivor, 77, 93, 107, 114, 117, 123
Avonmore Road, Kensington, 2

Bach fugues, 24
Baker, Mrs. W. M., 21, 59
Miss Mary Frances, 1, 2
William Meath, 104–6
Bakers, the, 37, 102
Bantock, Sir Granville, 44, 90
Bavarian Highlands, 2
Bayreuth, 2
Beauchamp, Lord, 115
Beaufort House (Gloucester), 77
Beethoven, 111
Berlin, 95
Berlioz, 123
B.G.N. (Var. No. XII), 101, 114
Birchwood, 10, 17–19, 30
Birmingham, 60, 80, 81, 90
Choral Society, 80
Festivals (1900), 32; (1903), 56;
(1906), 75; (1909), 88; (1912), 99
University, 76
Black, Andrew, 75
Black Country, the, 75
Black Knight, The, 2, 9, 120
Borland, J. E., F.R.C.O., 68
Boscobel, 7, 8
Brewer, Dr., 34, 93
Briggs, Rawdon, 90
British Camp, the, 16, 60, 62, 114
Brodsky, Adolf, 57
String Quartet, 57, 80
Brown, Herbert, 90
Buckley, R. J., 120–1
Burley, Miss, 11

Buths, Professor, 29, 33, 34, 45–9

Cadenabbia, 76
Cadenza, the (Violin Concerto), 95, 96
C.A.E. (Var. No. I), 12, 100–2, 116
Cambridge, 104
Caractacus (sketches), 8; 11, 17
Story of, 16
Cardigan Bay, 69
Careggi (Florence), 83
Cernikoff, Vladimir, 95
Chair of Music (Birmingham), 76
Chopin, 52
Cincinnati, 69
Cipher, 129
Coates, John, 55, 75
Cockaigne, 35, 36–7, 68
College Road, Upper Norwood, 1
Cologne (1904), 60
Colonne, M., 34
Colwall Tunnel, 61–2
Corfu, 63
Coronation Ode, The, 50, 52
Coronation of King George V, 97
Coronation Honours, 98
Così fan tutte, 11
Covent Garden Opera, 2, 105, 109
Craeg Lea (Malvern Wells), 10, 14, 15, 116, 127
Crossley, Miss Ada, 68
Crown of India, The, 98

Dan, the bulldog, 80, 113
Danks, Mr. and Mrs., 77
Miss Amy, 60, 91–4
Davos, 76
Decorations and Honours, 128
Devonport, 77
Dorabella, 11; (Var. No. X) 13, 112;
(published separately) 15, 28
Dunstall Hall (Wolverhampton), 8
Dunstall Park races, 7, 8
Düsseldorf, 29, 33, 34, 45

E.D.U. (Finale. Var. No. XIV), 16, 115–16

Index

Edward Elgar (R. J. Buckley), 120
E.E., 2, 4
  his whistle, 116
Elgar as I knew him (W. H. Reed),
  88
Elgar, Birthplace House, 108, 127–8
  Carice, 2, 11, 25–6, 63, 88, 90
  Caroline Alice, 41, 101
  Edward, 1, 122
    Visit to the U.S.A. (1911), 96
    Mus.D. of Cambridge (1900),
      33
    Lady, 8, 86, 124–5
    Sir Edward (1904), 62; O.M. (1911),
      97
Elgar-Blake, Carice, 53, 86, 120,
  128
Elgar Festival (Covent Garden 1904),
  49, 57, 59
Elgars, the, at Düsseldorf (1901), 45;
  (1902), 49
  at Gloucester Festival (1910), 91–4
  at Hasfield Court, 11, 37
  at Hereford Festival (1909), 88
  at Wolverhampton, 1, 4, 7–9
  Move to Craeg Lea, 14
  Move to Plâs Gwyn, Hereford,
    63
  Move to Severn House, Hamp-
    stead, 98
  Visit to the U.S.A. (1906), 69; the
    U.S.A. (1907), 76; Careggi
    (1909), 83
Elman, Mischa, 95
Elwes, Gervase, 90
Enigma, the, 23, 28, 119–21
Enigma Variations, 90, 117, 121
Ettling, E., 49, 55

Falstaff, 99
Felsnaptha soap, 50
Ffrangçon-Davies, 75
Fitton, Miss Isabel, 9, 107
  Mrs., 107
Florence, 83, 89
Forbes-Trefusis, Major the Hon.
  Henry, 115
Forli (Malvern Link), 6, 115
Foster, Muriel, 49, 75, 99
Froissart, 55
**Funeral March (*Diarmid and
  Grania*),** 68

Gerontius, The Dream of, 25, 31,
  35, 39, 52, 55, 58, 83, 88, 99
  sketches and proofs, 17–19, 21–2,
    28
  production of, 32
  at Düsseldorf, 45, 49
Gilbert and Sullivan operas, 123
Gloucester Cathedral, 94
  Festivals (1898), 11; (1901), 37;
    (1907), 77; (1910), 91
Goetz, Mrs. Ludovic, 77
Grafton, Miss May, 77
Great Malvern, 17, 22, 45
Green, William, 35
Greene, Plunket, 77
Griffith, Arthur Troyte, 9, 107–8,
  117–19
G.R.S. (Var. No. XI), 101, 112–14,
  117
Gürzenich Concert Hall (Berlin), 60

Hanley Festivals (1896), 4–5; (1903),
  54
Harley House, Hereford (1909), 88
Hasfield, 1, 2, 102, 105
Hasfield Court, 11, 37, 77, 103
H.D.S-P. (Var. No. II), 103
Heale, Miss Helen, 77
Heidelberg, 2
Hereford (Plâs Gwyn), 8, 61–2
  Choral Rehearsals, 80
  Festival Rehearsal (1903), 55
  Festival (1909), 88
Hiawatha (Coleridge-Taylor), 27
Higley, William, 75
'His Excellency', 11, 29, 65
Hodgson, Mrs., 29
Holm Lacy, 65, 110
Horse-racing, 8
Hull, Dr. Percy, 113–14
Humour and Harmony (Cernikoff), 95
Hyde, Mrs., 9, 106, 108, 117
  Miss, 108
Hydes, The, 12, 25, 35

Imperial Hotel (Malvern), 57
Indian furniture, 41, 63
In Hammersbach ('Bavarians'), 8, 9
Intermezzo, the, 15, 20, 21, 112
In the South, 61, 68, 69
Introduction and Allegro, 66–9
Italian Lakes, 76

Index

Jacques, Edgar F., 68
Jaeger, August Johannes, 13, 21, 23, 25–8, 37, 49, 55–6, 83, 109, 110–12, 124–5
Jaeger, Mrs., 83
Jaeger Memorial Concert (1910), 89
Johnstone, A., 46, 48

'Keeper of the Archives', 41–3, 79, 99
Kempsey, 119
Kingdom, The (sketches), 69–72; (production), 75–6, 77
King Olaf, 4, 5, 9, 42, 90, 113–14
Kirkby Lunn, 34
Kite-flying, 7, 111
Kreisler, 91, 94–5, 96

Leeds, 23
Lessman, Dr. Otto, 33
Lett, Phyllis, 90
Letters, from E.E., 4; (Mar. 1898) illus. 4, 11, 14, 15, 17; (Oct. 1901) illus. 38, 38, 39; (Oct. 1902) illus. 51, 52, 54, 66, 74, 78, 89, 96–7; (1903) illus. 124
Letters from Lady Elgar, 54, 69
Letters from A. J. Jaeger, 28, 29, 32, 33–4, 45–9, 59, 78–9
Lippspringe, Westfalen, 76
Llangranog, 69
Lone Pine (Townshend), 104
Lower Rhine Festival (1902), 49
Lux Christi, 8
Lygon, Lady Mary, 114–15

Maeterlinck's dramas, 121
Malvern, 44, 60, 108–9, 116, 120
Malvern Link, 1
Malvern Wells, 10
Marches, Pomp and Circumstance in D, 35–6; in C minor, 68; in G, 36
Marloes Road, Kensington, 1
Marseilles, 54
Mass in B minor, 57
Max Mossel, 113; (Quartet), 67
McNaught, Mr. W., 125
Meistersinger, Die, 105
Messiah, 58, 94
'Moods of Dan, the', 113

Music Makers, The, 98–9
Muswell Hill, 78–9, 87

'Nanty Ewart', 37, 102
Netherhall Gardens, No. 42, 98
Nevinson, Basil G., 103, 114
New Cavendish St., No. 58, 89
Nicholls, Agnes, 75, 90
'Nimrod', 13, 25, 28, 76, 78, 81, 83, 87, 98–9, 101, 117, 126
Nimrod (Var. No. IX), 65, 109–12
'Nimrod and Dorabella', 56
'Ninepin, the', 9, 13, 25, 57, 61
Noble, T. Tertius, 90
Norbury, Winifred, 9, 108–10, 120
North Hill, Malvern, 6
Novello & Co., 125–6

Order of Merit, 97
Original Theme (*Variations*), 121
Ottley, Miss, 1
Oxford, 88, 103

Parsifal, 123
Pendock (Worcs.), 1
Penny, Miss, 7, 129
Phoebus and Pan, 123
Plâs Gwyn, 61, 110, 127
Poker-work, 10
Portraiture of Variations, 100, 101
Postcards—from A. J. Jaeger, 60, 76 from E.E., 60, 66, 76, 96

Queen's Hall, the, 81, 94
Queenstown, 96

R.B.T. (Var. No. III), 12, 103–4; 20, 88–9, 101, 112
Red Gauntlet, 37
Redmarley (Glos.), 1, 41
Reed, W. H., 88, 92, 93
Revolving bookcase, the, 53
Rheingold, Das, 105
Richter, Hans, 14, 29, 33, 88
Richter Concert (19 June 1899), 100
Ring, Cycle of the, 105
Ripple Lodge, Malvern, 1
Roberts, Caroline Alice, 1
Roberts, General Sir Henry Gee, K.C.B., 1
Roberts, Lady, 1
Rochester, 81

Romanza, the (Var. No. XIII), 101, 114

Ronald, Landon, 99

Rope Walk, a (Wolverhampton), 9

R.P.A. (Var. No. V), 106–7; 100, 117

St. James's Hall, 100

St. Matthew Passion, 123

Sanford, Professor S. S., 65, 68

Scenes from the Bavarian Highlands, 8

Schuster, Mr. Leo, 77, 93

Sea Pictures, 23, 55, 68, 90

Severn House, Hampstead, 98, 99

Severn, river, 1, 2, 50

Sherridge (Worcs.), 108

Sinclair, George Robertson, Dr., 80–1, 112–14

Songs of the Sea (Stanford), 77

Spanish quotation (Violin Concerto), 86

Steuart-Powell, Hew David, 103

Stoke-on-Trent, 4

Stonechat, 61

Strauss, Richard, 123

Strong, Mrs., 89

Symonds, Rev. William, 1

Symphony in A flat (sketches), 38; 79, 81, 88

Symphony in E flat (sketches), 89; 96, 99

Tchaikovsky, Fifth Symphony, 56

Tenderfoot in Colorado, A (Townshend), 104

Tenderfoot in New Mexico, The (Townshend), 104

Terry, Professor Sanford, 92, 93, 94, 98

Townshend, Richard Baxter, 103
Mrs. R. B., 77

Townshends, The R. B., 88

Trefusis, Lady Mary, 115

Troyte (Var. No. VII), 13, 74, 101, 107–8, 117–18, 128

Turtle-dove, the, 84–6, 127

Uncle Remus, 103

United States, the, 69, 76, 96

Valma, Hélène, 35

Variations, the, 12, 14, 15, 20, 21, 23

Variations (rehearsals), 28, 34, 56; 88, 89, 99, 112, 115, 116, 117
at Düsseldorf, 34
composition of, 100, 101–2, 113
Finale, 125
piano duet arrangement, 114

Variations (personalities), 16, 21, 100–17

Villikins and his Dinah, 124

Violin Concerto (sketches), 85; 94–6
Rehearsal, 91; 92–3; 94–6

Wagner, 105

Walküre, 'fire-music', 10

Wand of Youth, The, 112

Webb, F. Gilbert, 68

Westminster Arms, the, 61

Westminster Cathedral, 49

Whinchat, 61

Williams, Mr. Lee, 93

W.M.B. (Var. No. IV), 13, 20, 23, 36, 88–9, 101, 104–6, 128

W.N. (Var. No. VIII), 108–10, 117, 128

Wolverhampton, 1, 9, 25, 44, 78, 129
Choral Society, 9, 44, 45
Floral Fête, 90
St. Peter's, 6; Rector of, 1, 20, 58–9

Wolverhampton Wanderers, 2, 4

Wood, Henry J., 34, 44, 46, 82

Wood, Sir Henry J., 96

Worcester, 19, 23, 30, 31
Brodsky Quartet Concert, 80
High School, 1
Festivals, 20, 77, 79, 108, 117, 127
(Philharmonic Concerts), 9, 12, 14, 15, 25, 35, 49, 75, 108
(Star Hotel), 20

Worcestershire Beacon, 6

Worthington, Mrs. Julia H., 86, 93, 94

Wüllner, Franz, 48
Ludwig, 46

Wye, river, 65, 69, 80, 110

Yale—U.S.A., 69

Ynys Lochtyn, 69

York Festival (1910), 90
Minster, 90

Ysaÿe, Eugen, 95

Ysobel (Var. No. VI), 101, 107

PRINTED IN
GREAT BRITAIN
AT THE
UNIVERSITY PRESS
OXFORD
BY
CHARLES BATEY
PRINTER
TO THE
UNIVERSITY

Pro